AF264244

# The Picasso Mirror

## Jean Gilbert

Hamilton, New Zealand
www.roguehousepublishing.co.nz

**The Picasso Mirror**
First Edition 2020

Published by Rogue House Publishing Ltd.

Copyright © 2020 Jean Gilbert
jeangilbert.com



The events and conversations in this book have been set down to the best of the author's ability. Some names and details have been changed to protect the privacy of individuals. Written permission to use the interview material has been granted by all those interviewed for this publication.

ISBN: 978-0-473-50340-6

Edited by Chad Dick (100percentproof.co.nz)
Cover design by William Dresden
Illustrations © 2020 Jean Gilbert

# Contents

# Foreword

Like Jean Gilbert, I suffer from Face Blindness: the inability to visually recognize people, even close friends and relatives. I see a woman in a cool *Doctor Who* shirt and want to tell my sister, only to discover it *is* my sister. I meet friends unexpectedly and excuse myself to the restroom, where I can check social media links to work out who they are. I meet colleagues I've known for years at a conference and introduce myself as if we are strangers – then do it again two hours later!

Like Jean, I was unaware of my condition until I was an adult. For years, I thought I was just bad at remembering names and faces. Maybe I was anti-social. Possibly I really didn't care about other people as much as I thought. That's certainly what those with Face Blindness are often told.

It was an enormous relief, in my late thirties, to learn I had a brain difference and that it even had a name – *prosopagnosia*. Suddenly, so many things made sense: why other people are so much better at small talk than me (they know straight away who they are talking to), or why moviegoers believe in plots I found far-fetched, like recognizing a character seen in a bakery again on a train. I wasn't just a self-centered jerk! I had a legitimate reason to struggle.

Now I am open about my condition, with the intention of avoiding awkwardness. But the reaction can be frustrating: "Oh yeah, I'm bad at faces too." Let me reassure you that not recognizing people out of context is perfectly normal for everyone, and our difficulties go beyond that. Face Blindness affects feelings and emotions, relationships, memories, dreams and ambitions… It would take a book to explain the impact the condition has on a person's life.

This is that book.

Not everyone wants to admit they have a dysfunctional brain. Not everyone wants to expose their life and struggles to scrutiny. Not everyone wants to learn the details of how others see them.

In *The Picasso Mirror*, Jean Gilbert bravely explains what life is like when you don't recognize even your own reflection. With humor and insight, she uses her own memories and notes, as well as interviews with friends, family and colleagues, to explore what life is like in a recognizable world full of unrecognizable people. Her story will help people with Face Blindness, or who know others with the condition, to better understand its implications and effects on every aspect of life. It will also inspire and encourage those with this, or any other, disadvantage in life, to live life to the full regardless.

Laura VanArendonk Baugh
www.LauraVAB.com

# Introduction

I am a writer. The genres I write are science fiction and fantasy. Novels, short stories, and screenplays. All of them are fiction. That means make-believe. So what possessed me to write a book about real life?

It all started on a car ride over the Kaimai Ranges. A writer friend, Lewis, and I were on our way to a writers' meeting in Tauranga. We had an hour and a half to fill. What better way to spend the time than by getting to know each other better.

Lewis is a storyteller by trade. His life has been full of hilarious escapades and gut-clenching experiences. These he draws from to entertain his audiences, both young and old. He has an amazing way of telling a tale that grabs you and holds your attention.

On this particular trip, Lewis was telling me stories of his life, both comical and a bit scandalous. (I may not remember the comical ones. It's the scandalous ones that stick with me.)

I listened with rapt attention until he turned to me and asked, "So what's up with this Face Blindness thing?"

*I gulp. Inside I'm frantic. My brain goes blank. I try to dredge something up, but I have no markers, no prompts to draw from. Where do I begin? What can I say that will be as interesting as his crazy life?*

"What do you want to know?" I asked, stalling for time.

That was how it began. The one question opened a floodgate. What is Face Blindness? When did you know you have it? Do you mean that if we met on the street, you wouldn't recognize me? Really?! What about family members? How did you meet someone and marry? What about your family in the States? Would you recognize them if you saw them? You get the drift.

Some answers I knew. Other questions took me by surprise, and my answers reflected that. I had not realized I was doing certain things until Lewis pointed them out to me.

Over a couple of years, more of our conversations revolved around the Face Blindness subject. The questions became more intimate. The answers were enlightening for him and me. Lewis tried his best to understand what it was like to live with Face Blindness.

One day, Lewis said, "You should write a book about it."

"What would I write?" I scoffed.

"About your life," Lewis said.

"I like writing about worlds I can control. The plot I draft by my hand. I design the characters and their course in the make-believe world. My life is boring. The plot is uncertain. I control very little. Who would want to read about my struggle with Face Blindness?"

"I would. It's very interesting."

I chuckled, not believing him. Yet, here we are. A book is in your hand. I guess Lewis's fascination with it changed my perspective. I hope you find this subject as interesting as Lewis did. If nothing else, it will give you a better understanding of what those of us with Face Blindness have to cope with behind our friendly smiles, and hopefully make you appreciate the simple things that most take for granted, such as friendships and love.

The people quoted in this book have been interviewed by a neutral party. I am grateful for their willing participation in this project. Their thoughts and perceptions have been, for me, a mixture of surprised enlightenment and sadness – of lost opportunities and past misunderstandings and of the constancy of true friendships and real love. It makes me realize that I am not alone.

How it makes my heart glow to know that even if I cannot recall it, I am loved.

A Picasso Reflection

One:

# Prosopagnosia

*"Who in the world am I? Ah, that's the great puzzle."*

*Alice in* Alice in Wonderland *by Lewis Carroll*

I can't see your face. No, it's not blindness in the sense that my world is dark. I can physically see that you are standing right in front of me. I know you have two eyes, a nose, and a mouth and even hair for those of you who have it. Not that any of those things matter. Even as I look upon you, I do not 'see' you. There is no image of your face in my mind. Once I turn away, I have no recall of what you look like. Nothing. It is as if you were never there.

Strange, isn't it? Not to see someone in your head? I didn't think much of it for a long time. I concluded that everyone saw the world the same way I did. The brain is both fascinating and puzzling. It has the capacity to do many wonderful things in the face of adversity. It will adapt to issues and install elaborate compensatory mechanisms without the owner even realizing it. I figured I had a problem with remembering names. But it went much deeper than that.

You might have heard of Prosopagnosia before. The lay expression for it is Face Blindness. The medical term comes from the Greek 'prosopon' meaning 'face' and 'agnosia' meaning 'not knowing.' Prosopagnosia (try saying that three times fast) is a cognitive disorder of face perception in which the ability to recognize familiar faces, including one's own face (self-recognition), is impaired, while other aspects of visual processing (e.g., object discrimination) and intellectual functioning (e.g., decision making) remain intact.

~

I didn't discover that I had Face Blindness until my late twenties. It was a television show that opened my eyes. I can't remember the title, only that it was one of those hour-long news shows such as *60 Minutes* or *20/20*. The show was about a brain disorder called Face Blindness. Though I had most of the symptoms, I pushed off the idea that I had it: wouldn't I know from the beginning that something was wrong?

That was my reasoning.

However, the show stayed in my mind.

A few weeks later, I was at the doctor's waiting room with my one-year-old. The new *Redbook* magazine was on the side table. I flipped through it, and lo and behold, there was an extensive article featuring – you guessed it – Face Blindness. I read it with a bit of skepticism until I reached the list of twenty-four symptoms. As I went down the list and checked off more and more symptoms, my heart started to race.

"Could this be me?"

I left the doctor's office and went directly to the store to buy a copy of the magazine. At home, as I reread the article, my hands shook.

The logical part of me screamed, "This is me!" The emotional part of me refused to believe it. Who wants to admit that there's something wrong with their brain?

It is difficult for people with Face Blindness to recognize that they have a problem because people with normal facial recognition don't discuss their reliance on faces. They take it for granted, just as I have taken it for granted that everyone was like me – seeing no faces.

At that time, there hadn't been much medical research on the topic. What was known was that there are two types of Prosopagnosia:

The first type is caused by some form of brain damage such as from a head trauma, a stroke, or a degenerative disease. Before the injury, the patient had normal facial recognition abilities that then became impaired. Because they have experienced facial recognition in the past, they quickly notice their impairment.

In contrast, those like me, who have developmental or congenital Face Blindness, are born with the disorder and simply fail to develop normal face processing abilities. It is in no way connected to normal intelligence and perceptual functions.

Only recently has research on Prosopagnosia been picked up by the medical community. Studies at Harvard University and University College London have concluded that about two percent of the population have some form of congenital Face Blindness: it affects about one in forty people. This suggests that millions of people may be face-blind. That's a lot of people! I find that fact both comforting and disturbing. Another interesting fact that has recently come to light is that there may be a genetic contribution to the condition.

There is a simple test now available that the general public can take, something that wasn't available until the late 2000s. I suggest you have a go and put your mind at ease. It was developed by the researchers B. Duchaine and K. Nakayama. The test is through the Birkbeck, University of London, and is called the 'Cambridge Face Memory Test.' You can find it online if you Google that name. It is used by researchers as a good indicator of whether a person has Face Blindness or not. I didn't come across it until years later; not that it would have made a difference to me. I already knew I had it.

Unlike a physical malady, such as a broken bone, a cut, or a bruise, Face Blindness is invisible. The problem is found deep in the brain. The medical profession only now is furthering their exploration into the physicality of the cognitive disorder. Research has recently shown that the two percent who suffer fall on a spectrum, in a similar way to those with Autism Spectrum Disorder. I fall high on the scale. It did not surprise me. After all, I don't even know my own face.

Though researchers are working to understand the mechanics of the disorder, the brain is a complex organ and a challenge to study. It will take years, maybe a lifetime before they have the answers, let alone a remedy.

Face Blindness has shaped my life, who I've become, how I view people and relationships, and where I think I am heading.

Keeping silent about my condition has not helped me in the least. In fact, it has been more of a hindrance. Emotional backlashes have filled my life, situations that could have been avoided if others had been adequately informed. Thus, my hope is that this book will not only educate those interested in the subject but also help families and friends of anyone with the disorder.

I hope to instill in all a deeper understanding of the nature of this condition, how it affects friendships and relationships, and offer some practical solutions to a few of the underlying problems that those like me have to face.

But most of all, I want to inspire others who may suffer from a disadvantage, whether it is Face Blindness or any other condition, to reach for their dreams regardless.

Think of it as a Picasso painting of real life. We may not all see things in the same way, but we can still see true beauty in that life that is worth striving for.

Two:

# Childhood

*"Without leaps of imagination or dreaming, we lose the excitement of possibilities. Dreaming, after all is a form of planning."*

*Gloria Steinem, journalist, feminist, activist*

Of the two types of Face Blindness, I have developmental or congenital Prosopagnosia. It means I was born with the disorder.

I grew up in the central part of New York State: apple country. Rolling hills and pristine lakes. The summers were short. The winters were long, with huge dumps of lake-effect snow isolating most of the area.

Our house was in the country about four miles from the closest town, Waterville. Waterville had a grocery store, a dentist, and a small doctors' practice. We even had a volunteer fire/ambulance department. Most of all, the residents were proud of the brand-new high school on the outskirts of town.

All your needs were taken care of in this small country town, but that didn't mean no one ever went to Utica, the closest city, about twenty minutes away. The industrial sectors of Utica and New Hartford, a suburb, supported the workforce of the whole region, including my father. The mall was there too. Not that we went when I was young. That came later when I started to earn money at thirteen through babysitting and cleaning jobs.

I come from a large family: three brothers and two sisters. I'm the third in the pecking order. Of the first four, I was the quiet one – the one that caused the least problems – and thus needed little attention. You know the label: the easy child. That was until my youngest brother, Jeff, came along and stole the title away from me. Looking back, Jeff's behavior patterns ran very similar to mine: quiet and reserved and, like me, no friends.

Even as a little girl, I found it difficult to make friends. It didn't mean that I secluded myself. I wasn't the outsider: that kid that everyone made fun of or shunned. No, I wasn't one of those. I knew that there were children who liked me. And there were many children that I liked, too. I would have been happy to have any one of my classmates as a friend – to be like the other girls. Yet, year after year went by and I had no girlfriend, no lasting bond of a lifetime friendship. I used to get jealous when others formed attachments. They laughed and giggled together, whispering secrets in each other's ears as little girls do. I know now that those girls have grown up and left school, keeping their bonds of friendship, which were formed early on, even into adulthood.

During those early years, I craved friendship like every other child. Humans thrive on companionship, and having friends is the way a child learns to interact with others. They start to understand how they fit into the world. Though a child's concept of what that 'world' consists of is limited, that world, and those in it, play a critical role in their physical, mental, and emotional development. For me, that companionship just didn't exist.

To my parents, I was just a quiet, reserved child. That I felt disconnected from society and that this was related to my problem with remembering people was not a link made by them or by me. Communication on the subject was non-existent. How can a child articulate such a complex emotional concept? It would have been impossible even if I had been aware that there was something 'wrong' with me. But that never crossed my mind in those early years. How could it? Not seeing faces was all I knew. I had never questioned that there was another way to recognize people. Even now, it's hard enough for those in the medical profession to understand the intricacies of the disorder, let alone leaving a child to figure it out on their own.

That said, there was one particular boy that stands out in my memory. His name was Brian. (I had to look this up in the school yearbook because I couldn't remember it or what he looked like.) He was a farm boy, from the next village over. I don't know why he stood out from the rest. He must have made more of an effort than the other children. Or, I might have fixated on him, concentrating my efforts of friendship on one individual. At this point, I can only guess.

From kindergarten to graduation, Brian was the one constant person in my life outside my immediate family. Even now after all these years, I acknowledge that fact, which is quite telling of our relationship.

You could say that Brian and I grew up together. We rode the same bus all through the school years. In the classroom, Brian sat next to me when we shared the same class in the first, fourth, and fifth grades. I was painfully shy and didn't talk much. Brian didn't seem to mind.

In fifth grade, we were in a production together. It was an English class assignment – a play. I didn't want to do it. I couldn't explain to the teacher why I didn't want to participate, just that I was very shy. The teacher said I had to participate, so I obeyed though I was terrified. Brian helped me. Maybe he saw my insecurity. Can you imagine trying to act with Face Blindness when you can't recognize people? As long as I could hear the students' voices and they did what was planned on the stage, I was okay. But if there were a deviation of any sort, for example the placement of a person, I was lost.

It's odd how it's only Brian that I remember. Even when I pulled out the old yearbooks while working on this project, no one else stood out. All those faces that looked back at me in those photos were all strangers. How can this be? Like Brian, we all grew up together. Logic tells me that there must have been others who had befriended me. But I have no evidence to back that up.

I don't know if the shyness was due to my disconnection with people because of my lack of facial memory or if it was an inherited trait. Whatever the case, the brain disorder had a detrimental effect on my relationships with my siblings and classmates.

To fill the void caused by the loneliness, I spent my childhood creating imaginary friends. Interestingly enough, none of them were human. No faces to worry about. Unicorns, horses, wolves, dragons – they became my friends. For a time, there was even an imaginary ghost who lived in the chimney next to my bedroom. These creatures went on many amazing adventures with me, anything that my young mind could dream up. Those were the days of living with the sheer freedom of innocent expressions and joy, unhindered by the complications of the coming teenage years and those raging hormones.

When you have a friend, even an imaginary one, they usually have a name. That was not the case with my imaginary friends. A name wasn't necessary. Again, I find this interesting. What mattered at the time were the shared adventures and the companionship. Since I lived in the country, the adventures tended to center on the woods and

go from there. Whatever 'friend' I was with didn't say much. I think that was because I didn't have much experience with how to communicate. The adventures were about the discovery of new creatures and the actions that followed.

These 'friends' got me through my youth. Bedtime was something I looked forward to. My mother must've thought me a strange child. Off I'd go, snuggling into my pile of blankets, to start another adventure with my companion of choice.

When discussing this period of my life, people have said to me, "You come from a large family. Surely, you must have had at least one sibling you were close to."

"Yes, and no."

Let me explain.

Though my siblings were a constant presence throughout my childhood years, I never felt a close bond with any of them. The first four of the six were born within five years. The two youngest came along much later. We didn't have much to do with them. I am the third – the middle child.

Yvonne, my closest sister, was sixteen months older. You would think that would've made us close. That was so far from the truth. We had such different personalities that we clashed through most of our growing years. She was vivacious, outgoing, and a girly-girl – all qualities I secretly envied. I was the quiet tomboy – jeans and t-shirt, hair in a ponytail with bangs hanging in my face. There wasn't a feminine thing about me. I'm not saying I didn't try. Believe me, I did. Yet, the tomboy in me always won. I felt comfortable wearing that skin.

At twelve, I had my long hair cut into a bob with bangs. It was the fashion at the time. It was courageous of me to try something out of my comfort zone. But my motivation wasn't pure. My sister had gotten the same haircut before me. She looked amazing! I was so jealous. Why couldn't I be sophisticated too? I thought if I had the same hairstyle, I would have the same sophistication. Boy, was I wrong.

There was no transformation like you see in the movies. You know the ones I'm talking about; the awkward tomboy teen turns into the gorgeous beauty queen. Instead, I felt exposed and soon grew my bangs long enough to hide my eyes behind them. I used my hair as a shield, looking at others through it thinking that they couldn't see me. That way I could observe them in the disguise of my shyness and not have to reach out and communicate. I don't know if this was a coping mechanism that my brain had set up to compensate for the Face Blindness. Interestingly enough, I kept the same haircut all through school.

Since my sister and I didn't get along, that left my two brothers. They had to contend with their pesky sister tagging along, getting into all sorts of pranks with them. Sure, they complained at times, but for the most part, they were good sports about it. We had many adventures in the hills around our house. I made sure I kept up with them. Sometimes, I even surpassed them when it came to rough-housing.

I think they must've sensed my desperation to belong. I'll give you an example. One day, before a planned trip into the woods, my brother Brian and a neighbor boy, Mike, took me aside.

"If you wanna be one of the boys, then you need to go through an initiation," Brian said.

I knew they were up to something. But I was desperate to belong.

"Okay," I readily agreed.

"You have to eat a worm," Mike said with a grin.

A worm. No big deal. I've eaten worse.

"I can do that," I said and bent down to search under a rock.

"No," Brian said. "We get to pick the worm."

From a rusty can, Brian pulls out the biggest nightcrawler I had ever seen. It looked like a rusty brown rope. He dangled the worm in front of me. It stretched down with the weight of its body, squirming, growing longer as I watched horrified.

"You can't be serious," I said.

"Totally," Mike said with a nod.

Brian held out the worm for me to take. "Yup."

I took the worm by its end. It twisted and turned as it tried to escape. I stared at it. Both boys waited in anticipation, grinning from ear to ear, so sure I was beaten.

"The whole thing," Brian said.

They had forgotten how stubborn I was and how much I longed to belong.

So, I did what anyone in my position would do.

I dangled the worm over my open mouth and dropped

the whole thing in. Without chewing, I swallowed the entire worm. It clung to my throat, gripping the sides with its segmented body. I tried not to gag. I gulped again and again, forcing it further down all the while feeling the rope of its body fighting to go up. Finally, it was down.

I opened my mouth wide to the boys. They stared back in astonishment.

"Guess I'm in," I said with a shrug and walked away.

When they finally caught up to me, my brother slapped me on the back in comradeship.

"Welcome to the club," he said with pride.

From then on, I was viewed as one of the boys. I liked that idea since my attempts at femininity had failed. Though Brian and Mike didn't realize it, they had fulfilled my young heart's need to belong, even if it had cost the life of a worm. I was happy. Poor worm, the sacrifice of your life was not in vain. I thank you, even now.

Country life suited me. Along with my brothers and the next-door neighbors' boys, we'd spend time after school, building forts in the woods and exploring the hills. Those were good times. When I think of those memories, it's not the person or people I see, but the activity. Things like making snow forts in the winter and sledding down the massive hill by the cemetery on anything we could get our hands on. We'd explore the woods and creeks. In the autumn, we'd have rotten vegetable wars and crabapple fights. Then there were the times I learned how to shoot a rifle and ride a dirt bike, the times we sneaked into the neighbors' houses to have a nosy-look. (That one wasn't my idea, but I didn't say no. It was so naughty and exciting.) I could go on and on…

Then came high school, and everything changed.

Three:

# Teenager

*"You don't get to choose if you get hurt in this world… but you do have some say in who hurts you. I like my choices."*

*Augustus in* The Fault in Our Stars *by John Green*

Adolescence. Ugh! I shudder just thinking about those years. High school was a world unto its own. For a shy thirteen-year-old, it was a challenge and not without its hardships. Add in the ongoing problems that come with having Face Blindness, and you can imagine the difficulties a young person like me had in fitting in.

Let me refresh your memory: someone with Face Blindness doesn't recognize other faces, doesn't remember the person/people after the fact. They can remember events, but not the people in the events.

Now, place that person in high school. The stresses of acquiring a good education have moved up a level. Expectations have become higher. Combine the pressure to succeed academically with newly raging hormones, and you have a recipe for disaster. Friendships change. Attraction to the opposite sex flowers. Romantic relationships are formed as students pair off. Then there are the breakups and the subsequent gossip.

Even now as I sit here typing, I can picture the high school in detail. A brick structure lies spread out on a hill with a parking lot on each end. I can see the inside with the partitioned walls, the open-box lockers, the suspended ceilings, the labs, music room, and gymnasium. All of it: the entire layout, including the grounds.

But when I try to put my classmates in the picture, I get nothing. Only empty rooms with unoccupied desks. If I try to remember the teachers, I can pull out forms – slim or fat – but no identifying features. With anyone. I can insert a figure into the classroom and assign the person a gender, and say, "That's Mr. Ryker, our math teacher," but it doesn't make him the real thing. I can remember award ceremonies, concerts, and dances. Who attended? I don't know.

Having friends became more critical during those teenage years. I knew I was shy. I decided to make more of an effort and worked hard to reach out to a few of my classmates. I tended to gravitate to those who were talkers. It was easier to let them carry the conversation than for me to voice an opinion.

There was one girl in particular. Her name was Deidre. (I had to look up her name, too. And no, I didn't recognize her face in the senior class photo. Doesn't matter. I didn't recognize mine either.) We had much in common: both from large families, both from low socio-economic backgrounds, both high achievers, and most of all, both desperate for friendship.

Those were blissful days. Finally, I felt like there was someone for me. We hung out together for most of the seventh and eighth grades.

Then, something happened.

A new girl arrived at school and joined our little circle. Her strong personality was the type that didn't share friends. Not long after, the two broke away. Deidre stopped hanging out with me altogether. I was crushed. There was no explanation when I desperately needed to understand what went wrong. I thought I had done something. It was only later when we were juniors that Deidre admitted she hadn't been strong enough to insist on including me in their circle. But the damage had been done, and there was no fixing it.

After Deidre, I tried a few other times but found the friendships petty and shallow. So, I gave up on having a girlfriend. They just didn't work. I figured it was because I felt I had nothing in common with them. All they talked about was boys, clothes, makeup, and oh yes, boys again, to which I had nothing to add. It was all so tedious. Plus it reminded me of my impoverished background, and I didn't need that.

However, I had no problem with the boys. I may not have said much, but I always had something to contribute to the conversation. I knew about hunting, sports, and outdoor activities. A typical tomboy. I maintained the same temperament – easy going – which my male classmates seemed to appreciate.

All the while, I never thought I was different in the sense that my brain didn't 'see' and remember faces, that the Face Blindness disorder was the reason for my trouble in making and holding friends. Yet, there was something inside me that kept whispering, *What's wrong with me?*

My brain knew the answer but had no way of telling me.

I knew, in general, I was liked by all. However, I was craving something more, something that was intimate, a relationship that would make me special in someone else's eyes, like I had experienced with Deidre.

What about Brian from elementary school? In high school, our friendship changed on my side. I really liked him and wanted him to notice me as girlfriend material. We were casual friends, not close, or should I say, not close enough for me. Brian was one of the popular boys. He had a charming personality, which made him very likable. Girls surrounded him, even the older students. So, how could I ever dream that he'd single me out?

In the ninth grade, to my surprise and delight, Brian asked me out to a school dance.

Finally!

I was in heaven.

*This is it*, I thought. *I've made it. I am normal. Someone likes me!*

I made a dress. It was blue with a small floral print. The dress had a drawstring at the waist and a V-cut neckline. I was so proud of that dress. I thought I looked good in it.

I was fifteen.

That night I experienced my first kiss. After the dance, Brian gave me his watch to hold onto. I floated all the way home. I couldn't wait until Monday.

"Brian likes me. As a girlfriend!" I confided in my sister, Yvonne, that night, hoping for some sister bonding.

"Good on you," Yvonne said. She had many boys flitting around her, like hummingbirds around the syrup bowl.

That was about the extent of that conversation. I didn't care. I was on a high.

From that night, I thought everything was going to change. With Brian as my boyfriend, I was going to be in the 'in crowd.' I was going to have someone who cared about me, who had singled me out from all the other girls. I would be loaded with new friends. All because of Brian's attention.

I was wrong again. Very unrealistic expectations, but you have to remember that I was only fifteen.

Though Brian was fond of me, he couldn't resist the charms of an older student. I was too shy to fight for him. I gave him his watch back and disappeared into the background, feeling rejected and lost. He never knew how much it hurt me.

I wondered about Brian's life long after I married. To this day, I still think of him once in a while: one of my few lasting memories. No, I don't see his face. If Brian were to come up to me now, I wouldn't know him from anyone else. Even when I look at his picture in the school yearbook, I don't 'see' him in the photo. It's such a strange feeling of disconnection, not just with him but with all my classmates.

The best way to describe the feeling is to imagine yourself arriving at a party and not recognizing anyone, yet being aware you somehow know them, even if you have no memory of them.

It is very disconcerting.

Because I didn't feel I fitted in anywhere, I had developed very low self-esteem. You would think this might have adversely affected my grades. It had the opposite effect. My concentration on my schoolwork intensified. (I'm a 'Type A' personality: organized, perfectionist, and a workaholic.) My academic expectations for myself were of the highest level. I demanded nothing less than an A+ score in all my subjects. If I failed at friendships, I was determined to succeed in all my classes and to outsmart all of my classmates. Of course, this was a formula for disaster.

Though I scored high in my classes throughout high school, even accomplishing those A+ grades I worked hard to acquire, I couldn't keep them up in every subject. When a final grade was less than my expectations, I took it hard, blaming my stupid brain.

In doing research for this portion, I pulled out my report cards from school. I had kept them all these years along with some awards. I wanted to verify that the grades were as I remembered. They were. I surprised myself, even now: I was a *good* student. But it wasn't enough to make me happy. They didn't fill that human need to belong.

After Brian, there was no other interest from my male

classmates. I should rephrase that: it was me who *perceived* a lack of interest from my male classmates. I learned later, at our fifteen-year class reunion, that a few did have crushes on me.

"Why didn't you do something about it back then?" I asked at the reunion.

One response was, "I thought you weren't interested."

The others nodded in agreement.

"You seemed unconcerned with us guys," another said.

"Come on, guys; I was shy!" was my automatic response.

We laughed it off as growing pains and lost opportunities.

However, knowing what I know now, I wonder if they weren't partially right. Did I come across as uninterested? What about the girls? Was it the same with them? Because I had become self-contained by then?

If only we could go back in time and observe, how much we could learn about Face Blindness and how it shapes who we are. There is a reason I say that, because during these difficult years, on top of the persistent loneliness, I had developed an eating disorder. I thought if I were thinner, people would notice me and like me.

I wasn't fat. Far from it. I was very active and fit.

It's not that I didn't know my classmates. I was in the same school system all my educational years, from kindergarten to my senior year. The average number of students in my class was about sixty-five to seventy. I grew up with these kids. I spent years doing homework with them, sharing the same gym classes, sitting at their tables during lunch and study hall, going on field trips. You'd think that I would have a connection with them or some long-lasting friendships. But, no. For that part of my life, there is nothing. I left high school with no associations attached. It was as if that part of my life never existed.

Oh, I remember the events that happened to me during

high school. Some of them are burned into my memory. Such as the time I was goaded into stealing a pumpkin for a Homecoming float and tripped over a wire holding a sapling. The tree snapped, and the pumpkin went rolling. Everyone laughed but me. I didn't dare say that I had hurt my ankle. I just picked up the pumpkin and limped along.

Then there was the time I'd nearly set the school on fire in lab class when the Bunsen burner had been left open on full blast by the last student. I didn't think to check it first and lit it. The flames shot up to the ceiling burning a panel before the teacher rushed over and shut off the main gas valve. I got a scolding on safety in front of everyone. It was mortifying.

Or the time the gym teacher teased me over my crush on my seventh-grade science teacher – right in front of the teacher. I thought I had done such an excellent job of hiding it, too. Another humiliation. How they must have chuckled at my innocent crush.

Anyway, you get my drift.

The eating disorder escalated as my feelings of loneliness persisted. When I looked in the mirror, my eyes saw an ugly, chunky girl staring back. I blamed my troubles on her. I didn't recognize her as being me – the 'internal' me.

The eating disorder became my way of gaining some control of my life where I felt I had none. It got so bad that I knew I was going to die. I had to stop but didn't know how. The eating disorder had taken over my life. Food became my enemy.

That part of my life was kept secret. I grew skilled at hiding the signs.

However, my poor health must have shown through, for my mother arranged a doctor's visit. I knew I needed help and so I told the doctor exactly what was going on. I think I shocked him.

Anorexia/Bulimia Nervosa were relatively new problems,

and there wasn't much information out there on treatment. I know that now. However, the doctor didn't know what to do with me, so did nothing, which made me feel worse – like I wasn't worth the effort to help. It was only after I met my future husband that I received the emotional/mental support that I desperately needed on so many levels.

None of my classmates knew of my internal struggles with a lack of self-worth and loneliness. Communication between my parents and me was insufficient: almost non-existent. I didn't feel secure in revealing my emotional state to my mother. I don't think she would have understood, just like that doctor. We lived in the country. My mother didn't drive. Any choice of cultivating a relationship with a peer was almost impossible.

Besides the two next-door-neighbor boys, a family of five girls moved in a mile away when I was thirteen. One was a classmate. Her name was Kathy. I always felt she was out of my league. Kathy had what every teenage girl dreamed of having: blond hair, blue eyes, and the perfect figure. Plus, these girls wore makeup and did their hair with hair products and blow dryers.

I was a late bloomer: a boyish figure, no makeup, no stylish hairdo. Just a 'plain Jane', especially in comparison with Kathy and her younger sister, Johanna.

I so desperately wanted these girls to like me.

Kathy and Johanna tried their best to be nice, but we had little in common. I felt it every time we were together. The friendship with those sisters was shallow and caused more harm than good.

When I was sixteen, I met a new guy visiting from Indiana: Jeff. He was eighteen and out of school. We had a lot in common, both being the outdoors type. We spent the summer hanging out together with my two brothers. I was hooked on Jeff. He, too, had blond hair and blue eyes, and his southern accent to my New Yorker's ears was divine. For two months Jeff was mine. Then, he met Johanna, and that was it. It didn't matter that Johanna had nothing in common with Jeff beside the blond-hair, blue-eyed thing. She was beautiful. When you're young, that's what's important.

I felt I had learned two lessons from that experience: 1) Friends are not all they are cut out to be, and 2) Don't expose your inner feelings. You'll only get hurt. I can't say that was the correct way to deal with the situation. I was young and immature.

That was my last attempt in high school at having a real friend. It would be many years into my adulthood before I would try again.

As for the eating disorder, it only got worse. Feeling like a failure drove my need for control higher. The one thing I could control was what went into my body. My parents still didn't have a clue about my struggle with food.

I became really good at fake eating. At one point, I was down to eating a piece of gum a day and the bare minimum for dinner. The only reason I ate at all was that we always ate dinner together as a family.

We were small eaters in comparison with other families. This was partly because we were poor and there were many mouths to feed. A typical dinner might consist of a hot dog on bread served with macaroni, or a small hamburger and some peas. Maybe a potato. We didn't complain. It was all we knew. It became easy to cut up the food and push it around on the plate or slip it into a napkin.

For years as an adult, I regretted that I didn't ask my mother for help, that I didn't explain how terrible I was feeling physically and emotionally. She may not have understood the eating disorder or the reasons behind it, but she loved me and would have done everything in her power to help.

To this day, my parents still don't know how close they came to losing their daughter. By the time I was sixteen, I was throwing up four times a day. Whatever I ate had to come out. I had an aversion to any food entering my body. I hated it. I hated my weakness for eating it. I hated myself even more.

In my sophomore year, I took up field and track sport. I was an average runner. I didn't have the drive to be the best like I did with my education. Besides, my health was on the decline because of the lack of nutrition. By then, I had been starving myself for over a year. It made running difficult, to say the least. By my senior year, I had no energy left and had to drop out. I didn't care. To be honest, by this time, there wasn't much I did care about.

My eyes developed blood blisters from the pressure of vomiting. I couldn't look at anyone because they would see them. So, I kept my eyes down until they disappeared. My heart pounded like it was working overtime. Palpitating. I could barely function; I felt lethargic. My limbs trembled with weakness. I wanted to die. No one would miss me. That was my reasoning. I was invisible to them.

Those were dark years.

~

Those days are a distant memory. In this case, Face Blindness has been a blessing. The people associated with the past are not remembered. The horror of that period is gone. It takes enormous concentration to recall any of it. As I write this, there is a feeling of sadness for that time, but no sense of loneliness. No pain. Just a sorrow for the lost opportunities.

With no real connections with my peer group, and with a couple of bad relationship experiences, I relied heavily on my imagination for companionship. The unicorn, horse, wolf, and ghost were retired onto the shelf of my childhood. I was ready for some more adult-themed adventures.

Creatures were replaced with people. Usually, it was a boy. He was introduced somewhere early in the story. As the adventure progressed, the boy turned from being a friend into something more. This is where I experimented with talking to boys, imagining me as another character – like an actor. That character became someone I could control in both behavior and conversation. At a time when my own life felt like it was spiraling down into a bottomless pit of darkness, I fell in love with that creativity and the sense of control it gave me.

The material for my fantasies came from books, movies, and real life. Sometimes, depending on my mood, the adventure would take a dark turn. It was a way to explore those dangerous paths without harming myself, and a way to work through those teenage feelings without having a support person to confide in.

Did it help? To some degree, yes.

Designing scenarios and characters takes hard work and much forethought. Creating those scenes and playing with dialogue through those transitional years laid the foundation for what was later to become a writing career. It kept me occupied at a time when I could have done more damage to myself.

Throughout high school, I remained a high achiever. My grades never faltered. A few months before graduation, I had to switch schools because I had moved out of the area to Warrensburg, deep in the Adirondack Mountains of New York. The reason was because I got married. I know: what was I thinking?

Most young people would have balked at the prospect of starting in a new school, especially when so close to finishing, but not me. Maybe that's an advantage to having Face Blindness – everyone is new each day.

When Warrensburg High School received my transcript,

they questioned my grades. They thought the transcript was forged. No one gets one hundred percent and on so many subjects. The teachers had never seen anything like it before. The guidance counselor called my old school to verify that the transcript was real. When they were told it was correct, they didn't know what to do with me. The school had no classes to offer me that I hadn't already taken. I thought it was quite funny. I ended up cruising through the last three months of school. The new girl became the valedictorian, and they had no idea who I was. I felt sorry for whoever it was that I had usurped. It wasn't fair, and I knew it but couldn't do anything about it.

Four:

# The Classmate – Dan

Gamora: *What do you do with it?*
Peter Quill: *Do? Nothing. You listen to it. Or you dance.*
Gamora: *I'm a warrior and an assassin. I do not dance.*
Peter Quill: *Really? Well on my planet, there's a legend about people like you. It's called… Footloose. And in it, a great hero, named Kevin Bacon, teaches an entire city full of people with sticks up their butts that dancing, is the greatest thing there is.*
Gamora: *Who put the sticks up their butts?*

Guardians of the Galaxy – *screenplay by James Gunn & Nicole Perlman*

School, an important era of life, ended. I had spent almost thirteen years at the Waterville schools – elementary and high school. But all those people I grew up with were no longer a part of my life. As soon I moved away from the area, all my classmates were forgotten – erased. It was as if that portion of my life had never happened. Logically, I knew it had.

Somehow, leaving everything familiar behind – the school, my classmates, and the memories (or lack of memories) built around them left me feeling free. Everyone I met was truly new to me.

Only since social media came onto the world scene have I reconnected with a few of those old classmates. I follow them on Facebook but rarely reach out to them. They are strangers. Only when they post an old photo from school, do those memories come back. Not of the people, though, but of the events surrounding them.

However, just to be contrary, something made me want to connect with one of my former classmates when I knew that I was going to be in Washington D.C. on one of my trips back to the States. His name is Dan. I discovered he was living and working close to the convention center where I would be attending Awesome Con 2017[1]. Dan didn't know how difficult it was for me to reach out to him, the battles that took place inside my mind. Yet I was glad I did, especially when Dan kept saying how smart I was. Am! I still am! That's one way to boost a person's ego.

When I first went through the tape that the interviewer gave me and listened to Dan's point of view, it blew me away. How he saw me was so different from how I saw myself. I missed so much because of this brain disorder.

~

Jean and I were friends in elementary school: the third grade, to be exact. That's a long time ago. Waterville Elementary was a small school. Most people didn't move away. So the same kids grew up together. Each year, our class would be pretty much like the last year. Jean was a regular.

In the summer, our school sponsored swimming lessons for the students. Jean lived out in the country. Our bus would go by and pick up her, her younger brother Roger, and her older sister Yvonne. We'd take the bus to Colgate College in Hamilton to use their pool. It was about a half-hour drive to

---

[1] Awesome Con is an annual pop culture convention in Washington, D.C., similar to the International Comic Con held in San Diego, CA. The annual event has become one of the largest fan conventions on  the East Coast of the United States. See *awesome-con.com*

the university. Jean and I sat together on the bus. So, yes, I did get to spend time with Jean. She was always a really nice person. And really smart. She was funny, had a good sense of humor. And did I mention smart? (laughs) Yeah, real smart.

When we entered high school, Jean and I shared a lot of the same classes, spent a lot of time in the same places. Like the elementary school, Waterville High School was considered a relatively small school. Our class, if I remember right, was around 50 to 60 students. Jean can correct me later if I'm wrong. You get to know everyone. It doesn't matter the grade. Under or over, you knew them, and they knew you. I knew Jean pretty well by this time.

My social position in high school was somewhat awkward. My father was the principal. You can imagine what that's like, being the principal's son. (laughs) I'm joking. It wasn't too bad. Yes, he was kind of a disciplinarian. And even though people generally liked him, he had a tendency to rub people the wrong way once in a while. Sometimes, I'd get teased, but, hey, I survived.

Also, I was a nerd before nerds were cool. I had a lot of friends, but they were the more studious ones. Jean was one of them. She was a nerd too. Don't get mad Jean; nerds are cool now!

Jean's social position was the same as mine. She was a really good student. Education mattered to her, to us. She had a lot of friends. We weren't big party people. We sat together at lunch. We'd hang out as a big group especially when it came to high school – Tim, Dean, Kim (Jean's future sister-in-law), and a bunch more. We had the same outlook. That doesn't mean we didn't joke around with each other. We were kids. Kids do stupid stuff. It was fun. Jean would joke right back.

Speaking of nerdiness – Jean was a really good student. I

know I keep repeating myself. Academically, she was the top of our class. She ended up graduating in a different high school right near the end of the school year because she got married. I think Jean would have been Valedictorian, otherwise. She was right up there. Really smart.

It was well-known that Waterville High School was considered an academically gifted school. We had several from our class alone go off to Cornell University and Clarkson University, just to name two. Other classmates went to top universities around the country. So, it wasn't easy to be the top student of our class.

Jean was definitely superior. I can remember one time we went to the Oneida County spelling bee. Jean won it and qualified to go to the New York State spelling bee. For some reason, Jean couldn't go. I was runner-up, so I went. And lost in the first round. Good times in Mr. Allen's English class, remember Jean?

Jean was quite fun to be with and a warm person. I can't ever say that she seemed distant. She was a good friend. I remember standing in the lunch line and talking about different things. She knew a lot of stuff and was very interesting. Yes, I would say, Jean was reserved to a certain extent. Maybe even shy. I was loud at times. We were all nerdy. I chalked it up to that. Not that Jean was in any way different. Jean was popular among our group of friends. We all liked her and got along. She was always a kind person.

I know what you're going to ask next. You've put me on the spot. I did ask her out at one time. I think most of the guys in our group wanted to ask her out. I don't know what happened with them, but for me, she kindly told me that because of her religious beliefs, she couldn't go out with me. But we were still really good friends. I was also interested in going out with Kim, too, but she rejected me also.

Overall, looking back at our school years, I can honestly

say that there was nothing about Jean that made her stand out as different. Not socially, or anything else.

After graduation, I saw Jean only at the class reunions. The last one was our fifteen-year reunion. There was a long stretch in between. We were all married. It was funny because it was the same nerds at the same table just like old times. It never changes. We had to laugh.

Then came Facebook. I don't know if it was me who connected first, or Jean. Sometimes old classmates would post pictures from school on their pages. I think that's how it happened.

Last year, Jean messaged me through Facebook, saying that she was going to be in Washington D.C. for a weekend in June. She had a booth at Awesome Con to showcase her novels. Jean knew that I lived nearby and wondered if I wanted to get together while she was in town.

We made arrangements to meet in her hotel lobby. I was nervous that I wouldn't recognize her. I didn't have to worry. Uwe, her husband, was there and grabbed me as soon as I came through the door. I knew Uwe from when Jean was dating him. He had come to a few of our school dances with Jean. I also remembered him from the class reunions.

I didn't know that Jean was nervous, too, and had arranged for Uwe to point out who I was because she wouldn't be able to recognize me, even with my pictures on Facebook.

When I found out that she had Face Blindness, I was intrigued. I didn't know it was a thing. Jean didn't tell me about it until months later when she had asked me to do this interview. Nothing gave it away during that dinner in Washington D.C. It was the same as when we were young. At dinner, Jean told me that I hadn't changed. On the phone later, she said to me that she couldn't remember what I had looked like at all, yet would say things to gloss over the truth so as not to seem weird. She called it 'coping mechanisms.'

The date and time for the interview were set up. The interviewer was from New Zealand, so it took some work to get the days right and the time. I think they are something like fourteen-sixteen hours ahead of us. A whole different day. In the meantime, I stayed away from looking up information on Face Blindness. I didn't want it to affect my answers. I only had a vague idea of what it was.

Looking back, I wonder if maybe Jean's shyness in class, even though she was always nice and got along with all of us, I wonder if it is possible that sometimes it was as if she was seeing us for the first time. Kind of like she knew everyone, but maybe wasn't sure who was who, and who was saying what. Perhaps that's why Jean had friends like us because some of us were boisterous – Dean and me – we were pretty loud, all about us in some ways. She could be part of the group, and it wouldn't matter if she were quiet, if she couldn't recognize us. I wonder if maybe the shyness was an effect of the Face Blindness. I don't know.

Even during the breaks, like Christmas vacation or spring break, I never noticed anything weird about Jean. During the summer, on the bus to swimming lessons, Jean knew I'd be on that bus. Maybe she took cues from her sister and brother. Jean would want to sit with her friends but maybe wasn't sure where they were. I was friends with her older sister, and maybe that was Jean's cue. I never noticed anything. Why would I? I've known Jean since we were eight.

Now, I am very intrigued by this Face Blindness. School was a long time ago. Jean wasn't pathologically shy. She was an excellent student, quiet in class. We had assigned seats. We sat in the same place every day. That probably helped her. I would think that the structure and regimen of school helped her to cope with the Face Blindness. Yes, I would describe Jean as more reserved than others, though that didn't stop her from having a good time and laughing. But there was never anything odd about her.

Back in the restaurant in D.C., Jean didn't give away that she didn't recognize my face. This was before she told me about the Face Blindness. When I talked about one of our mutual friends, Chris, I got an odd sense that she didn't know who I was talking about. I didn't realize, at the time, that Jean was deliberately using certain questions in order to figure out who Chris was. I find that fascinating. She told me later that she uses questions to direct the conversation. I had no clue she was doing that.

Jean gave me an example of how she manages with the Face Blindness. This is what she related:

"For example, last week I went to a work function put on by the private hospital I work in. It was held at a restaurant. There were thirty women there from all over the medical community. I look out on a sea of faces. I don't recognize anyone. Maybe I do know them. Maybe I don't. Some come up to me and say, "Hi, Jean," and I have to figure out where they're from within the medical community. But I do it. Fearlessly. That's what I do. That's what I have to do. Face Blindness doesn't limit me as far as putting myself out there. But it's true; I do have coping mechanisms in place. I have to figure out their name, how I know them, where they fit in my life. All without them knowing what I'm doing and as efficiently as I can. There are systems that I use. Questions I ask. Information gathered and sorted. I do it all the time. It has become second nature to me."

When Jean told me that, I was blown away. And she does this all the time. Amazing!

Though I hadn't seen Jean in ages, the conversation felt comfortable. Unforced. Nothing felt unusual about it. She had put me at ease. I was relieved. Now that I know Jean has Face Blindness, I would pretend not to be who I am. (laughs)

Maybe that's why she didn't tell me in the first place. She is smart, after all.

It's funny because I had recognized Jean even after all these years. She looks pretty similar to what she looked like in high school. It's interesting to me that when she looks at my face, she cannot recognize me. Or anyone.

The brain is very interesting. Lots of stuff goes on. How the brain can compensate and cope with things, setting up coping mechanisms without our knowledge is amazing. There may be a lot of people out there with the same issue but who don't develop as healthy a coping mechanism and then are not able to be successful in school, or are not able to do things. It's a real testament to Jean's being more intelligent than most – to cope with the Face Blindness, to compensate.

Imagine people who don't have the same intellectual capacity to come up with methods of coping. It would be quite difficult for them. They would tend to be introverts, especially if they are unaware that they are different. Maybe that's why Jean was attracted to fantasy books – because of the Face Blindness. Those worlds were not real, just like her world felt. It must have helped her think about things in a different way.

Before Jean told me she had Face Blindness, I knew nothing of it. Now I'm very interested in it. It struck me as the same type of thing as people who taste words when hearing or seeing colors sends a taste to their mouth. These people think everyone experiences that, but we don't. It's just the way that the brain picks up on things and processes information for them.

I've been thinking about Face Blindness since Jean told me about it. I am a schoolteacher. I wonder how many of the students I've taught through the years have had the same thing. Jean told me two percent of the population has Face Blindness. That's a lot of people. I knew that eight percent of the population has color blindness, which is a different thing. I think Face Blindness would be more difficult to live with.

Chances are that some of my students have it, and I didn't know. They didn't know.

It has opened my eyes to view my students in a different light. Maybe that's why a student acts a certain way or explains how they behave with other kids. There's more going on than we see with the eye or can reason with conformity. I plan on looking more into it now that I know and view my students with a different mindset.

Face Blindness doesn't hinder Jean. I can see that, all the way back from school and to what she does now as an adult. It amazes me because Jean has picked professions where she needs to know who people are. It's interesting that she doesn't limit herself because of the Face Blindness even though it's an uncomfortable situation for her. Jean just copes with it. She likes to help people, and it shows.

I'm glad to have done this interview. I really like Jean and am glad she reached out to me. I'm looking forward to reading her book. I'm sure it will help me to understand her better. Maybe I can use it to help my students, too.

Five:

# Dating

*"People think a soul mate is your perfect fit, and that's what everyone wants. But a true soul mate is a mirror, the person who shows you everything that is holding you back, the person who brings you to your own attention so you can change your life."*

Eat, Pray, Love *by Elizabeth Gilbert*

For someone with Face Blindness, self-containment becomes a way of life, a way of functioning. It's not on purpose. Humans need the interaction of others: the conversation, the physical contact, the memories. It is an innate requisite of our psyche.

Self-containment has three definitions:

1) Constituting a complete and independent unit in and of itself;

2) Not dependent on others, self-sufficient; and,

3) Keeping to oneself, reserved.

Think of the definitions when it comes to building relationships, not only through childhood but into adulthood, and how it changes the dynamics, even perceptions. Think about all the people in your life: your childhood friends, schoolmates, workmates, and lovers. The memory of them becomes a part of you.

I don't have that. I am missing those all-important

connections in my brain.

I can't remember my childhood friends, my teenage friends, even my family. No faces – no connections. This has made me self-contained, I think, as a preservation mechanism.

Think back to your youth and how important those relationships were to you – the good and the bad – the friends, enemies, and romantic relationships.

Sometimes I think it's a miracle that I ever found someone who could love me. I'm not saying that I didn't like guys. Remember, I was desperate to be liked. Being loved by someone of the opposite sex was a dream to me. Oh, how I wanted it! I wanted someone for my own, someone who would care about me, care for me. Yet, I had three significant faults that kept getting in the way – shyness, a sense of worthlessness, and the as-of-yet undiscovered Face Blindness.

So, how did 'love' happen?

I was sixteen when my older sister, Yvonne, started dating a young man from Bolton Landing, New York. The quaint town is located deep in the Adirondack Mountains, halfway up Lake George, a popular tourist destination. It was around a four-hour drive from where we lived.

With the towering mountains, the pristine lake, the scent of the pine-filled air, and stunning views, Yvonne and I quickly fell in love with the area.[2]

-------

[2] This particular area became one of the main settings in my young adult series – *Beyond the Wall. Light in My Dark* and *Light in My Blood*, the first two books in the series can be found on **Amazon.com.** Bolton Landing boasted the most beautiful of hotels called The Sagamore Resort. I changed the name of the town to Glen Eden and the hotel to The Hedemann House, making it a deserted mansion. The mansion gave the imaginary town a sense of mystery. The school in the book is real, as are some of the

My sister and I ended up making the long drive to Bolton Landing every other weekend. We didn't mind. It was a chance to get away from home.

On one of those trips, her boyfriend, Don, was invited to play basketball. Us girls went along. I loved playing basketball and wasn't that bad at it either. My sister, being a girly-girl, stayed on the sidelines. I didn't know the people I was playing with, only that they were Don's friends. One of them, a tanned, handsome young man, hit me hard in the gut with the basketball. That got my attention. You know how they say that boys will hit a girl to show that they like them... Well, it worked.

His name was Uwe. It's German and pronounced like Oova. I liked him right away. But after that visit, when we were back home, he was quickly forgotten. I had nothing, no anchor such as a face or memento to place him in that memory. I know that a guy hit me with a basketball and that we ended up talking for a bit after the game. I hadn't recognized any signs that he was interested in me even though they were there. I didn't look at people. Probably because my brain already knew that it was a useless exercise.

On the next visit to the mountains, Uwe was there again. We were at an event in Lake Placid for the weekend. Uwe and his buddies were attending too. On the first night, he asked me to dinner. It was then that I had the first clue that he liked me. I wouldn't go to dinner with him unless he invited the other girls that were traveling with me. To my surprise, Uwe did and paid for everyone. Wow! I was impressed!

Afterward, we talked for hours. We had so much in common: lots of siblings, growing up in the country, small-town schools, both liking outdoor activities and sports. His

---

features of the town. Bolton Landing was where my future husband grew up.

voice was like warm honey, the kind you can listen to forever. Radio friendly, I called it. It drew me in along with his gentle kindness and genuine concern.

At first, I was quiet. I didn't know how to communicate besides the mundane: sports, the weather, school stuff, places I'd been… To express any opinion or inner feeling was beyond my capability. When the conversation turned personal, I felt very vulnerable because of past hurts. I wasn't ready to expose my inner self to anyone, not even to this genuinely nice young man. It took hard work and gentle persistence on Uwe's part to get me to open up. It was one of the things that endeared him to me.

At the time of our courtship, neither of us knew anything about Face Blindness. Now, it's different. We've been married a long time. Uwe knows the details of the disorder. You can call it a first-hand education. Up close and personal. We both look back and can see how the disorder affected our lives. Some incidents were small. Some were astronomical.

When I went over his recorded interview, some of his perceptions took me by surprise. It brought home how much I honestly cannot 'see.' I blame my being self-contained and disconnected from people.

You may be asking how we ever got together when I cannot recall people?

What made our courtship work was our long-distance relationship. I know that sounds strange. Most couples would struggle with not seeing each other regularly. I agree that being together, seeing each other is a much better option than not having physical contact.

In today's society, we have modern technology to ease the long-distance problem. With the availability of computer programs such as Skype and FaceTime, seeing your boyfriend/girlfriend can be done instantaneously and at any time. The visual connection is maintained. The nuances of body language, along with the tone of voice and movement of the face, can help cement emotional ties.

The lack of facial recognition for someone like me makes these communication options of lesser importance. For example, my oldest son lives in the States. Though we regularly Skype, his face remains out of my mind. Any visible expressions that added depth to our conversations are gone the instant the contact is disconnected – wiped away as quickly as a switch of a light. The words may remain. At the time, I can say that he was happy, sad, upset – whatever emotion he was feeling. But without facial recognition including expressions, the memory of it disappears with the click of a button. It leaves me feeling neutral. Not happy. Not sad.

When Uwe and I were dating, I was still in high school and didn't have my own car. I had to depend on Yvonne to make the four-hour trip to Bolton Landing. When she got married, the car went with her and thus, my ride. Uwe worked full time and couldn't make the trip every weekend. We ended up seeing each other once a month.

To carry on dating, we both became very proficient at letter writing. I still have those letters – a whole box full! Little did Uwe and I know that this form of communication was the best thing for me. I had his picture. He gave me one when I asked for it. Yet it was the words and the emotions of the words in those letters that stuck with me and moved me. I could read them over and over. His face was gone from my mind as soon as he turned away or I shut my eyes. The letters were my grounding to him, a constant feature where I needed one. Not a visual one like a picture. My brain had already switched off from trying to recall faces. The letters were information that I could store away and process like a textbook. It became my emotional connection, something I needed far more than the memory of a face.

'He's tall... brown hair... did I say tall?'

As well as his words, it was Uwe's voice that was important. We made a point to talk on the telephone as often as we could afford. I listened to him for hours. These conversations etched his voice into my brain. At the time, I didn't realize that I depended on voices as a means of recognizing people. And I never questioned that other people didn't use voices too.

Before each visit, I would study that photo. I didn't understand why at the time. I thought it was out of anticipation. I know better now. I was trying to remember what Uwe looked like.

When we met up again, it wasn't Uwe's face I was focusing on. No, I was subconsciously tuning into his voice. In the end, it never mattered what he looked like. It was the memory of his voice that kept me joined to him, and the sincerity I found in those letters.

I kept all his letters and recently took their dust-covered box from the attic. When I pulled the letters from their envelopes, the paper was brittle in my hands. The writing was faded, yet I couldn't resist reading them.

During the nine months of our dating and engagement, Uwe wrote me seventy letters. I wrote eighty-eight. This was before emailing and texting. I was curious to see if my writing revealed anything pertaining to the disorder. (What's the saying: hindsight is twenty/twenty?)

Interestingly enough, the letters did. Looking back with the knowledge I have now, it's as plain as day. Where Uwe's were full of emotional expressions, mine fell short by a long shot. We were a couple in love! My letters should have been full of mushy lovey-dovey stuff: *I miss you! I love you! I can't wait to see you!* That kind of stuff.

Talking to other couples of my generation and their experience with letter writing, I realized after the fact that mine were neutral – stiff even. I knew that something was wrong with me when I tried to express emotions in those letters and found it forced and unnatural. Nonetheless, I had to write something even if it was only a paragraph or two, especially when Uwe's letters were full of sentiments of love.

Below are two samples – one from each of us. These letters were both written a month after we got engaged. On November 24, 1981, Uwe wrote as follows:

MY DEAREST AND <u>ONLY LOVE</u> JEAN,

I love you, Darling. I love you! I wish I could have seen you last night, but what could I do. I now wait for tonight. I hope you come up to the house today. I have to work late tonight, and after we get out of work, my father wants to go shopping. So, I'll be home around 8 o'clock. Oh, honey, if you only knew how extreme my love for you was. I don't know really how I express my love for you. When I see you tonight, I'm going to kiss you right away. I love to kiss you, you taste so nice to me. When I'm close

to you, I remember how much I miss you when you're gone. I can't take it, going more than two weeks without seeing you. Don't think that I <u>EVER</u> stop thinking of or about you because I <u>DON'T!</u> Honey, I want to make you as happy as any woman ever was. I want to share with you all of my love. I want you to want <u>only me.</u> I need you to <u>need only me.</u> Honey, I can't stop telling you that I love you, because I really love you. Honey, I want our love to grow continuously every day, more and more. Baby, I need you. Jean, share your life with me, and I promise to make you happy! I'll do all I can to make you happier than you've ever been. Darling, be my wife for eternity, let me love you now till always. Let's have our love prove itself. Honey, I love you. I have to go.
I love you.
All my love,
Uwe

Mushy gushy puts it lightly! Every letter from Uwe was about the same, a little about what he was doing and then, a lot about his feelings. Is that normal? I don't know. I dare not trust my own judgment when it comes to emotions.

The next letter is mine. This particular letter goes on for six pages. I'm starting on page five because that's where the first sign of any affection shows up. The pages before are filled with events of the week, so you aren't missing anything. The date on the top reads December 18, 1981.

Hello.

As you can see – today is Friday. (finally) It sure did take its time in coming, but I'm glad it's finally here. I should be studying for a couple of tests, but I'd rather write to you. <u>You</u> are more important to me.
It hasn't quit snowing since last night. I wonder how much snow we will end up getting. I hope you make it here okay! This morning, the roads weren't plowed yet.

They are kind of slow down here. We are supposed to get <u>five</u> new snowplows for this area. We really need them.

Oh, I can't wait to see you! It's been such a long time. I'm glad that you're coming today. I couldn't bear another weekend without you. I love you so very very much! I always will – forever. You make me so happy. I'm glad that I'm going to share my life with you. I'll need you always.

It seems like in <u>EVERY</u> <u>CLASS</u> I have a test today. (Thrilling) So far, I have taken a typing test and an English test. I've still got three more classes to go. (plus my studyhall) I'll manage. I always do. I think I'll only study for my math test.

I still haven't figured out the song you've been talking about. I've been listening to the radio, but I haven't really heard anything that might be it. I guess I have to wait and see which one it is. Which one is it?! I'm so curious.

No more time to write. Sorry about that. I love ya forever. Remember that. I'm glad you're coming.

Forever yours,
Jean

One paragraph of affection out of six pages of exposition. What makes this exceptionally noteworthy is that I was newly engaged at the time of the writing of that letter. You would think that I would've been spewing words of love and affection and thoughts of our future together. No. One paragraph. Just one.

Face Blindness sucks. It really does!

While going through my letters to Uwe, I found names of

people I now have no recollection of who they were. It seemed at the time I knew them quite well, for I had private information about them that I had shared with Uwe. The handwriting was mine. The logic of the writing was mine. Yet, it was like the letters were from someone else. Reading them felt like I was invading this other person's privacy. Such a disconcerting feeling, especially knowing that it was I who wrote the letters to begin with.

The good news out of all of this is that letter-writing worked for me. Though I had no idea that I was dealing with Face Blindness through our courtship, somehow I formed an attachment to Uwe. A dependency. Finally, someone loved me, and I couldn't be happier.

But I use the word 'attachment' instead of 'love' in describing my personal feelings for Uwe. There's a reason behind this careful choice of words.

# Six:

# The Boyfriend – Uwe

*"I am nothing special; just a common man with common thoughts, and I've led a common life. There are no monuments dedicated to me and my name will soon be forgotten. But in one respect I have succeeded as gloriously as anyone who's ever lived: I've loved another with all my heart and soul; and to me, this has always been enough."*

*Duke in* The Notebook *by Nicholas Sparks*

The first time Jean and I met, I was in my senior year in high school. I had the lead role in the school play – a comedy called *May the Farce Be With You*. Jean had come to the show with her sister who was up visiting my friend, Don. After the show, Don introduced the two girls to me. We talked for a few minutes. I instantly thought Jean was the prettier of the two. If you ask Jean about that first meeting, she will tell you that she can't remember me, only that the lead character had a fake mustache that kept falling off and that he was funny.

My oldest sister lived in Virginia with her husband who owned a commercial construction company. My brother-in-law offered me a job when I had finished high school. I decided to take it and left New York soon after graduation. His company focused on building chain restaurants such as the *Red Lobster*. Work soon dried up, and he started looking to move the company elsewhere. Texas was booming. We ended up in the Houston area, which I loved.

Though I liked working in construction, after two years, I was ready to do something else. My father heard and sorted me a position at the print shop where he was employed. I took it. Soon, I found myself back home where I met Jean again. We ended up playing basketball. She will tell you that I hit her with the ball. That's her side of the story. I don't remember doing that. Maybe I did. Whatever the case, I got her attention. After the game, we all went out for food. We talked for a bit. I liked her.

We met again a few weeks later at an event in Lake Placid. She had some friends that she hung out with, but I could tell that they weren't close friends. She kept a lot to herself, you could say, on the sidelines. She mostly hung around her sister and her few friends.

One evening, we talked late into the night. I knew she was shy, yet, I found out a bit more about her. I really liked her. That's where it really started.

Jean told me later, after we were married, that she had me picked out for one of her friends. I wasn't interested. My eyes saw the girl I wanted, and that was it.

By this time, her sister was engaged to Don. Don invited me to go with him when he went to visit his fiancée. That meant a whole weekend spent in Jean's company.

I learned a lot about Jean on those visits. Jean was quiet. She loved being outside, going for hikes by herself, doing things by herself, being a tomboy. She chopped wood like a boy, played all the sports with the guys, and generally was very capable. Jean lived in the country. Rolling hills. Apple country. We would go for walks in the woods.

Jean and her brothers had built a cool lean-to into a hillside up in the woods about a mile from her house. A bunch of us would go there, light a fire, and hang out. I could tell Jean loved the woods. She seemed at peace, in her element, whenever we went for a hike or spent any time at parks, mountains, and lakes – any part that was nature.

At parties and gatherings, Jean was quiet. Her older sister was the complete opposite – loud and boisterous. I was drawn to Jean because she was very pretty and kind. And it didn't hurt that she liked sports.

I knew Jean was shy and didn't say much. That was okay. I was the outgoing one, and I think she liked that. No, I know she liked it. It took the pressure off of her. And I was happy to do that for her. In that way, we complemented each other.

We started officially dating that summer. One of the things Jean did right away was ask for a picture of me. I gave her one. I didn't realize until years later that she used it as a flashcard so that she wouldn't have to say, "Who are you?" She couldn't remember what I looked like. We only saw each other once or twice a month. The rest of our courtship was done through letters and many hours on the phone. You should've seen my phone bill! She was worth it.

Jean is good at figuring out personalities and listening to voices. She used to tell me (still does) that she loved my voice. It has something to do with the quality, pitch, and timbre. At the time, I didn't know that she relied on voices for recognition. I don't think she realized it either. It has only been since the diagnosis that we've talked about the possibility.

When I would visit, I never had the feeling that Jean didn't know who I was. She always knew when I was coming over because we lived so far away, and it had to be arranged. I wonder what her reaction would've been if I had unexpectedly shown up. That would've been an interesting meeting. Then again, once she heard my voice… the game would be up.

Then, there were my friends. Whenever Jean came up to

Bolton Landing with her sister, we'd all get together with my friends. We'd do things like hang out, play football or basketball, go out to eat… all the usual things young people do. In the winter, we'd ski, go sledding, goof around at the lake, play games or watch movies inside. A normal person would remember everyone's name by this point. Not Jean.

On one occasion, we went to my friend Kevin's house to play pool. It's not like Jean didn't know Kevin or his brother and dad. After the greetings were over, she'd lean in and ask quietly for their names again. I put it down to Jean being an introvert. I already knew that she liked to be by herself, that she found it difficult to be around people, afraid of being made the center of attention.

She never said, "Oh, I don't remember that person," or "Have I met them before?"

As a young person, I wasn't thinking of it as a medical problem.

I remember showing her pictures of a group of my friends. She'd ask for their names and if she had met them yet. I thought that was odd because she had already spent time with them. It made me feel like she wasn't interested in them. It was the same with my siblings. She had a hard time with their names. Not that they were difficult like mine, but more of putting the face with the name, remembering who was who, and even calling them by their name. At first, I thought it was because there were a lot of new people to remember. But, when time went by and she still had a problem remembering, I put it down to her having a lack of interest in my friends and family. Yet, that didn't feel right either. It's hard to explain. Jean was so kind and generous. She listened with real interest and got along with everyone. I couldn't gel the two behaviors together.

Talking to Jean was like pulling teeth. It took hard work to get anything personal out of her. But I wanted to know her and so pressed on. I noticed that Jean didn't look at people. I thought it was because of her shyness, only realizing later that it was because she physically couldn't remember anyone. It was a real thing, this Face Blindness.

Jean was very self-conscious. When she finally confided in me about the eating disorder and her feelings of worthlessness, I was blown away. Here was this smart, pretty girl, and she thought of herself as nothing. I had to do something about it.

By this time, we were engaged. Jean was already a thin person. She was very athletic. So, when she dropped to ninety-nine pounds, it was more than alarming. I was scared for her. I told her that I loved her, but I didn't want to marry someone who would be taken away by a gust of wind. I didn't realize how much that hurt her. How could I understand when neither of us knew about the Face Blindness and that it was the cause of her insecurities.

I decided to just be there for her. Be a constant in her life. A friend. Her best friend.

It worked.

Seven:

# Marriage – Part One

*"It is not time or opportunity that is to determine intimacy; it is disposition alone. Seven years would be insufficient to make some people acquainted with each other, and seven days are more than enough for others."*

*Marianne Dashwood in* Sense and Sensibility
*by Jane Austen*

Adolescence can be likened to a war zone: raging hormones, peer pressure, trying to work out your future. It's a minefield of potential disasters waiting to happen. Very few come through unscathed. Nonetheless, it's a journey everyone must take. When the transition from teenage to adulthood has been completed, we say, "Whew! I made it!"

Those high school memories and school friend relationships are slotted away to be looked upon, in later life, with a lingering fondness, or for some, with blessed relief that they had survived.

I became engaged to Uwe during my senior year of high school. Uwe and I had decided to marry in April. Yes, we were silly. At the time, I was desperate to marry. I look back and think, why didn't I wait until after graduation? I now understand why I pushed the wedding sooner. It wasn't for sex. (Well, maybe a little.) It was for something deeper –

something that I had longed for all my childhood and into my adolescence. I had found someone who loved me, even with all my insecurities. I was afraid of losing him, of losing that connection with another human being.

Face Blindness had made the decision for me.

Marriage bound us together – one human to another. A Vow. It provided a stable environment, structure, and a defined role. I settled right in, loving the fact that I had someone to take care of, someone that belonged to me. Oh yes, the brain disorder was still there but yet to be detected.

Uwe's memory amazed me. He could remember the finest of details about someone: what they looked like, where they came from, their connections, and relatives.

I thought, *Wow! I wish I had that kind of memory!*

I became heavily dependent on Uwe for names.

I'd lean in and whisper, "What was her/his name? Did we meet them before?"

He was always ready to fill me in. He never said I was stupid or forgetful.

"I wish I had your memory!" I'd complain.

He'd smile and hold me tight, saying, "That's what I'm here for."

It made me feel good. And Uwe, in return, felt needed.

We moved around a bit during our marriage. (Our children would protest at this point and say, "A bit?!" Well, maybe we moved more than a bit.) Uwe was an off-set printer by trade. After we married, we moved around New York State, not so much by choice but because of the job. The printing industry was moving out of the state due to the high tax rate.

In our sixth year of marriage, Uwe took a job in the central part of Illinois. Most of Charleston's twenty thousand population came from the students who attended the Eastern Illinois University attached to the town.

Illinois was a corn and soybean state. The sky went on forever. It was so flat you could see the curve of the Earth on the horizon. In the early autumn, the corn stalks turned golden, signaling the change of seasons. Miles and miles of endless golden fields. The yellow corn against the bluest of skies took my breath away, so vivid were the colors. I was used to mountains and trees, not this fantastic stretch of sky.

It was this move that gave me the first real eye-opener about my disorder. Uwe went ahead to Illinois, while I stayed back in New York and organized our things. By this time, we had two pre-school age children. I packed up the house and organized a truck and family and friends to help with the lifting.

At the other end, we needed a new home. That was Uwe's job. It took him a while, but he finally found one, two miles outside Charleston, perfect for a young family.

An eighteen-hour drive later, the children and I were reunited with their father. We had been separated for six weeks. We had never been away from each other before this time, not even for a day.

Right away I knew something was wrong.

We had made arrangements to meet at the storage unit where we were to temporarily store our belongings. The house wouldn't be ready for another two weeks. The men were waiting – about four or five of them. I didn't recognize any of them. This was before cell phones. I had no way of calling Uwe for verification – and no way to check on Google Maps.

I hesitated to get out of the truck. I rechecked the address. I was at the right place.

*Where is Uwe?* I thought, as the men came to the truck.

One of the men left the group and came directly to me. There must have been something in his face – a smile, a softening in the eyes – something that clued me in. However,

I wasn't sure until he started speaking and I recognized his voice.

"Uwe!"

The logical part of me told me that this man was my husband, but I felt no connection to him. It was weird. My husband was a stranger. All memory of our emotional connection was gone.

We kissed and hugged. It felt so awkward, like the first time you kiss a stranger. At that moment, I couldn't understand why it would feel that way. We had been married for six years! I could tell Uwe was confused about my odd behavior. He had a right to be. I was confused too. Yet, neither one of us broached the subject. After the initial greeting, we got caught up with our busy lives. Soon enough, the incident was forgotten…

We lived in the Charleston area for two years. Then, Uwe got a better job offer in Champaign, about an hour from where we were living. We found a cute farmhouse in the country outside the village of Weldon in DeWitt County. It was surrounded by miles-and-miles of cornfields. Our lawn was so big that the farmer would park his huge combine harvester on the far edge. The kids loved it. I did too. We planted a big garden. We had cats and dogs.

The desire to have a real friend was still there. So as soon as we moved into the area, we found a local church of our faith in the town of Clinton.

We both thought this would be a great place to make new friends with like-minded people.

They were friendly, I won't deny that, and maybe a little curious: we were a novelty of sorts being New Yorkers. I know that sounds odd, but in some ways it was true. Though I tried to make an effort and reach out, I hit a social brick wall.

When we moved away from the East Coast to the Midwest, we never expected a cultural difference. But the

United States is a vast country, full of diversity. To have different cultures within the country shouldn't have been a surprise. However, it took us both aback. We were young and ignorant.

Neither of us was prepared for a different way of thinking. I described it as 'small town syndrome.' The people live, work, die in their small town. Whatever happens outside that town holds no interest to them, unless it affects them personally. Coming from the East Coast, with our New York accents and fast-talking ways, Uwe and I stood out like aliens. Though we tried to make friends, it took years to feel welcomed, and we were never entirely accepted.

Needless to say, during our five years in the Midwest, I was very lonely: more so than at any other time before in my life. We had moved away from family, friends, and connections back east. I tried, believe me, I tried. But to fight against a social wall, with my handicap, was an impossible feat. I soon gave up.

I was heavily pregnant with our last child, Lane, when we made the move to the country home in DeWitt County. The birth was difficult and took a lot out of me. With two young children at home, a new baby, and the dogs, I was kept very busy. I was only twenty-seven, but I was exhausted and couldn't shake it off.

A year went by. Lane was a one-year-old when I saw the program on Face Blindness on television, followed by the magazine article with the list of symptoms.

I was shocked. This was me!

So much of my earlier life finally made sense. It was like a black cloth had been removed from my eyes, and I could see clearly for the first time.

Initially, I told no one what I had discovered about myself, not even Uwe. I needed reputable evidence. A television show and a magazine weren't enough.

Before the age of the Internet, sources for information were limited to the local library. We had a public library in Clinton. I borrowed the car for the day, got the two older children off to school, and with my youngest in tow, set off for town. Though the library wasn't extensive by any standards, it hosted plenty of resources. I rushed to the card catalog. I tried F for Face Blindness. Nothing. Then, P for Prosopagnosia. Still nothing. Disappointed, I carried my one-year-old to the desk and asked the librarian.

"Prosopagnosia? What is that?" she asked.

"Face Blindness. Where someone doesn't recognize other people, even family members," I replied. "Sometimes not even themselves."

"Oh! There was something on TV about it last month," she said.

I grew excited. "Yes, that's it. Face Blindness."

"Let me check."

I sat down with some books and tried to entertain the baby while I waited. Ten minutes later, she came back to me.

"Sorry. I couldn't find anything," the librarian said. "You could try the university library in Champaign. They may have some information on the subject."

Champaign, where Uwe worked, was about forty minutes from home. Though I came home that day disappointed, I wasn't ready to give up. I was sure I'd find something on the subject in the university library. The trip had to wait until the next payday when I was scheduled to get the car again.

The University of Champaign was a reputable college. Surely, their library housed the information (confirmation) I was looking for. How disappointed I was when all it offered was a few paragraphs in a medical textbook. I had learned more from the television program and ladies' magazine than from a professional medical journal.

The only other option was to visit my doctor. I took in the

magazine with the list of symptoms.

"I think this is me!" I said after he read the list. "Is there anything you can do medically to prove it?"

The doctor shook his head, "No. We know very little about the condition. Other disorders and diseases of the brain have taken precedence: Alzheimer's, Parkinson's, and the like. It may be years before any research becomes conclusive even on these."

"But, do you think I have it – this Face Blindness?"

"Going by this list and what you've told me, yes, most likely."

"So, there is nothing I can do? No cure?" I asked.

"Nothing at this time," he said. "I'm sorry."

Like the heavy blade of a guillotine, the confirmation cut me deep to the heart. Though there were no medical tests available besides a list of symptoms, the doctor was pretty sure that I had Face Blindness.

I stopped looking for answers.

Deep in my gut, I knew I had Face Blindness. There was no other reasonable explanation.

Weeks went by. I told no one what I was going through. I was alone in a new state. No friends yet, only my three young children. Uwe was still in the dark. I didn't know how to tell him that there was something wrong with my brain.

Like the loss of a loved one in death, the thought of having a brain disorder affected me the same way. I had already experienced the shock of discovery. Next came denial.

A brain problem? Me? I was smart! Competent. Logical. There was nothing wrong with my brain; I was sure of it. I tried to push the whole thing aside. But like an irritating itch, it kept niggling away inside my head.

More time went by. The denial gave way to anger. The more I thought about my past and the things I had suffered, the angrier I got.

"You took my youth away from me," I cried to the disorder housed inside my brain. "You ruined me."

My emotional state, the continuing eating disorder, the lack of friends, the loneliness… all caused by this stupid disorder! How dare it hurt me? I could have been someone better! I could have had friends like others. I could have been accepted. *Normal*. Oh, yes, I had reasons to be angry.

When the anger ran out, I was left feeling deflated. The churning of my heart cried for the lost opportunities, for the 'could have beens,' for a normal childhood. I so wanted to be normal.

But like the mourning process, these feelings soon lessened – although they never truly disappear for good. From time to time, something will trigger their revival. Longtime friends, not mine of course, but as an outsider observing humans interacting. Conversations about shared memories of people. Sitting alone in my home, writing, making characters interact and become friends, even enemies. It's more than I can do in real life.

Now that I had an explanation for my loneliness and disconnection from people, I was ready to move on. I made peace with my internal struggle. I accepted the disorder. I was who I was.

Even so, I didn't share the diagnosis with anyone, finding it embarrassing to discuss. In fact, I tried to forget it myself. However, each time I had to ask Uwe for a name, it brought it home again.

My marriage remained a constant feature. After the revelation, Uwe and I went on as before: Uwe in ignorance of my internal dilemma, and me trying to hide the fact that something was wrong.

I can't remember when I finally told Uwe about the disorder. It was some time when we were still in that country home in DeWitt County. I do remember that he took it better than I did. He saw the truth in it. In me.

His words were, "That explains a lot."

I had to agree because I had said the same thing when I found out. And that was it. No more discussion. I needed Uwe to understand. I think he thought he did. However, today, he will admit that he genuinely doesn't fully understand the disorder, and that's after living with me for years.

After the revelation, life went on – me with my lack of connection to people and Uwe with falling back into old habits.

During the time in Illinois, Uwe was hardly home. Work and other community responsibilities took most of his time and energy. I felt like I was raising our three small children alone. The feeling of worthlessness rose up from the depths of my soul and reared its ugly head once more. I felt out of control. The eating disorder returned. My health suffered.

I remember crying one day. I couldn't stop. I was sitting at the dining table. The children were there. I think they were

at my knees, crying too, not understanding what was wrong with Mommy. I couldn't comfort them. I was too lost in the dark recesses of my mind.

I hardly ever cried. I can count the times on the fingers on my hands. So, you can understand why this day sticks in my mind. I saw no way out. No freedom from the darkness.

I spoke of none of this to Uwe. Not of the return of the eating disorder, not of the feelings of worthlessness, not of the pit of despair that I was sinking into.

I blame it on an accumulation of factors. First was the strain of not fitting in. Second was my strong drive for perfection in life – house, children, yard, you name it – it had to be just so. Third was starting back to normal life too soon after giving birth to our third child. Fourth was the absence of my anchor in life – Uwe.

Uwe's parents had become unwell, and he needed to be close to help them out. By this time, Lane was almost three. We made the long trip back to New York with all our belongings, again stuffed in a *U-haul* truck.

I was so relieved to go back home. At least there, the surroundings felt familiar. You could say a grounding, not of people, but of places: buildings, mountains and lakes – things that were in my memory. Stabilizers.

Some people felt familiar too, which was a great relief. I relearned their voices, though I still didn't recognize that was what I was doing.

We lived with my parents for a few months until we found an apartment in Utica where Uwe worked. The apartment was small. We thought we could manage the lack of space, but with three children, it soon became apparent that it wasn't working. The next place was outside the city and close to a town called Remsen near Boonville. It was a three-bedroom house with a good size yard for the kids to play in.

Though almost three years had passed since Lane was

born, I hadn't yet recovered from the difficult birth. The emotional and mental stresses of the Illinois move, plus my physical weakness, took a heavy toll. I had put on a brave face for as long as I could, but the body eventually gave out.

I became so unwell that I couldn't function anymore. Not as a mother, nor a wife, nor a human being. A doctor finally diagnosed me with Chronic Fatigue Syndrome. I became a body without a mind. Just to function day by day became a severe trial. It took two years for me to get back on my feet, and more years to feel normal again. Even now, I have little recollection of those horrible years. All I know is that the children had to grow up fast. Though they were young, they did many of the chores around the house. I didn't even have the strength to raise my arms to hang the laundry or wash my own hair. I made food in the morning, something simple for dinner, and that was about it. The children learned to use the washing machine, hang the clothes, and take them down. They vacuumed, did the dishes, and dusted. The older ones were about nine and ten: the youngest was still under five.

The move back to New York and family was good for us. Neither Uwe nor I were happy in Illinois. But now, in familiar settings and culture, we found our feet again and our marriage was back on level ground. With the Chronic Fatigue affecting not just me but the children, too, Uwe had to re-assess our priorities. He had to step back from anything extra to hold our family together and help me to recover. The illness was a great teaching tool as to what was important and what was not. We were back to being a team again. A family unit.

That was one phase of our marriage. The children are grown now and have families of their own. Our marriage also has changed. Life never stays the same. If it has, then you must be dead, for death is the only factor that remains unchangeable.

Eight:

# The Husband – Uwe

*"You are my best friend as well as my lover, and I do not know which side of you I enjoy the most. I treasure each side, just as I have treasured our life together."*

*Noah in* The Notebook *by Nicholas Sparks*

At eighteen, Jean was her own woman. I knew it from the beginning. Though she was quiet, I could tell that she was mature even for how young she was. Jean has said through the years that I had helped her grow as a person, that I taught her how to communicate. No one else had taken that kind of interest in her. One thing you will quickly learn about Jean is that she doesn't like to talk about herself, especially her emotions. Even to this day, she will say that she's a loner, that she doesn't need people.

I liked her personality. Jean was self-sufficient, industrious. She knows what she wants and goes after it, but not in a loud way. It was easy for people to like Jean because she was always loving and kind. If she saw a need, she wouldn't hesitate to fill it. She's what I'd call a 'Fixer.' Someone who always wants to help other people, who finds a way to fix things. I think this has to do with her industrious nature.

Jean works hard. One of her pet peeves is procrastination.

She's definitely one that you can depend on to get things done and to be on time.

Her brain is always going. It blows me away. Always thinking. Always doing. I think that's one of the things that makes her a good writer. The writing has always been there. I can remember one of our first fights was over a story she had started to write. Before this, I had no clue that she liked to write, so I didn't handle it very well.

My background, when it came to reading and writing, was so different from Jean's upbringing. Her family read *a lot*! I'm not kidding. When we were dating, I'd come in the house and find everyone in a corner somewhere reading. My family weren't readers, so how could I understand Jean's love for books and the need to write.

One day, I came home from work, Jean was scribbling away in a notebook.

"What are you writing?" I asked.

"A story," Jean said.

"Can I read it?"

"I guess."

She reluctantly passed it over, knowing I wasn't big on science fiction and fantasy.

I quickly scanned it. It was a fantasy. Something about elves, I think.

I gave it back and called her story *stupid* and *unimportant!*

"Why are you writing that crap?" I demanded.

I crushed her so much that she put her writing aside. I was the one who was stupid and ignorant. Not Jean. I didn't realize it was Jean's way of connecting to the world and to people.

Only years later, did she pick it up again. How I regretted those hurtful words. Jean is a great writer. I'm so proud of her. I wished I had let her do her thing all those years ago. Who knows where she'd be today.

I knew my wife was unique. I liked that about her. Neither of us knew about the Face Blindness until many years into our marriage.

Like I mentioned in the dating stage, I could see signs of the Face Blindness here and there, but it was so little that I brushed them off.

Now married, we spent every day together. You soon become accustomed to how each other works and thinks. The first time I thought, *Hmmm… something's weird,* was shortly after we were married.

After the honeymoon, we settled in the mountains outside the tourist town of Warrensburg near Lake George. Dave and Linda, folks I grew up with, let us rent their rustic home that was tucked into a mountainside. The house was surrounded by wild blueberry fields. The woods were full of bears, drawn by the smell of the berries. Walks in the woods were a favorite pastime of ours. Along the path were large pine trees. Some had marks in the bark, a sign of bear country. The gouges were so deep that they revealed the pale wood underneath. We were always cautious when we went into the woods. One thing you don't want to do is scare up a bear. The bears came down at night and snuffled the ground below our bedroom window. Deer were a constant feature in the surrounding meadows.

We both loved it there.

I worked an hour-and-half away in Troy. Jean worked as a chambermaid at a local motel. Our house sat back from the road. Near the road was a large barn where Dave and Linda stored equipment and supplies for their wood stove/furnace business. Some of their more precious things were stored in the back area of the house. They came quite regularly to the house and the barn.

One day, when I came home from work, Jean said that someone had been in the house. She didn't know that it was

Linda. Dave told me later that Linda had come to the house to pick up something for the shop. Now, I must tell you that Linda had a very distinct look with her long hair and tall stature. Yet Jean insisted that she didn't know the woman and that she was alarmed. At the time I excused Jean for not recognizing Dave and Linda because she hadn't been there long, and I'd known them for years. I also knew that Jean hadn't been around many people before our marriage.

That was my first clue that something wasn't quite right. But like Jean, I brushed it off and forgot about it.

Then, there were all the times Jean asked for help with names. It was a constant thing. I thought Jean had a bad memory. She'd continually ask, "Who are they? What are their names?"

I remember everyone. Why didn't she?

She would say all the time, "My memory with people sucks," or, "Oh, you have such a good memory!"

Her words and pride in me built me up.

So I thought, *Yes, I do have an excellent memory!*

I didn't mind her whispered questions. I put her poor memory of people down to her growing up alone, reading by herself, and her having no friends.

However, if you asked me, I was a bit embarrassed for her.

There were Face Blindness signs all along the way. I never picked up on them. Why would I? Jean was so smart, the top student in her class. Sometimes it was intimidating. Probably some of it was due to her being so well-read, where I was not. She had no problem retaining knowledge – sciences, mathematics, movies, books. She was a storehouse of facts. Her sense of direction was always spot on. I'm one of those people who gets lost in the mall.

The first time I noticed something was really wrong was when we moved to Illinois. I took the job and stayed on while Jean went back home to pack up and get the kids. We were apart for six weeks.

When Jean stepped out of the *U-haul*, I thought she'd be so happy to see me. What I got was a cold reception. Her eyes were blank. Her hug felt wooden. I thought something was wrong. I was too afraid to ask.

Then, we got busy with the move. Soon after, I forgot about the incident. Things were back to normal, and life moved on.

Jean did tell me about the Face Blindness a few years later, but it didn't register what it meant. I think that was because she was so intelligent, and I was used to her asking for people's names.

Jean showed me the magazine article and said, "This is me! I think I have Face Blindness."

I looked at the article because she was so excited. I tried to be interested, but it was hard to understand it, even when it was set out in black and white – even with all the evidence of the past ten years of our marriage. I still have a hard time with it.

Jean really can't distinguish between people, even races. Jean is not racist in the slightest. So, please don't take this next portion wrong.

If you ask Jean, she will tell you that all black people look the same. Or Asian people. I used to make fun of her.

"Really? You can't see the difference in our black friends?"

"No. Can you?" she asked.

"Yes!" And then I go on to list the differences – eyes, lips, hair, cheeks, noses, skin tones.

I didn't realize that to Jean, it was true; they all looked the same – black. No variation. Just black. She never came out and said, "I can't see their faces." It doesn't matter the race, she has difficulty with all of them.

It wasn't until recently that it really sank in how much it has affected Jean's life. I never thought about myself in the equation. But I was not excluded which took me by surprise. To be honest, it did bother me more than I had expected.

A few years after we had emigrated to New Zealand, I went back to America to visit family. Jean had made the trip already. I was gone for a month. During that time, I had grown a mustache and lost some weight. When I got off the plane and went to meet Jean, I got that blank stare again. She didn't know me!

All the way home, Jean was angry.

"Why did you grow a mustache? You know I don't like them," she said.

It hit me that the mustache made me a stranger to her. She honestly didn't recognize me. That revelation floored me. That's when the Face Blindness became real to me. It took many years for me to say it out loud and to truly understand the realness of the disorder.

I can't imagine not being able to recognize people. People are everywhere, in every part of life. I think of family – Mom and Dad, my brothers and sisters. I think of friends, classmates, work mates. I think of actors on television and in the movies, or famous people of the past and present.

Just think about it: when you see George Washington on the dollar bill, you know who it is and the history behind that person. At a glance, we know the value of the bill. Jean sees a drawing of a man. That's it. She depends on the printed number to know the value of the bill. She knows who George Washington was and what he accomplished in history, but there is no connection to him and that dollar bill. And that's just one small example.

Jean didn't start talking about the disorder and how it affected her life until she discovered her youngest brother, Jeff, has Face Blindness too. It was the first time I realized the severity of the disorder. Jeff falls higher on the spectrum. He can't remember people or dreams. He easily loses the facet of family and love. Talking to Jeff gave Jean clues to her own struggles. From then on, she started looking back. When asked, Jean told me she never spoke about the Face Blindness because she didn't want to draw attention to herself. Her brother was the catalyst that made Jean look into it more. Now it was a legitimate problem. It helped me become more aware of it and encouraged me to help her more with people in day-to-day life.

Knowing that the Face Blindness was a real thing and experiencing it through Jean's life, I was able to observe with amazement how Jean functions through what could be awkward situations for her. She has learned through a lifetime of knowing what questions to ask, what to say, and what to hide when conversing with someone. In the meantime, her mind is racing to figure out who they are: a friend? A family member? A new acquaintance? It must be exhausting, yet her face remains happy and her tone light. Then, something will click inside, most likely from the voice or something the person is wearing, or body posture, even tattoos. Never the face! Not at all!

Has Face Blindness affected our relationship?

How can it not? It has made us the unit that we are. Though neither of us knew about the Face Blindness until later years, it didn't change the way I felt about Jean. I have always been there for her. I'm always willing to help her. I love her. I didn't care about her difficulties with people. I put it down to her poor memory.

I couldn't understand why people didn't like Jean or didn't want to be around her too much. I had my buddies. Jean had no one. No close girlfriend in school or as an adult. No one who she really bonded with.

From day one of our relationship, she'd say to me, "I'm a loner. I like to be by myself." Or, my favorite, "I'd rather spend time with my cat."

At the time, I didn't understand. And yes, if I'm to be honest, it was frustrating.

"Why don't you want friends?" I'd keep asking. "Everyone wants a friend."

I'm a people person. I like getting together with friends, playing sports, going on trips together, or having a meal together and enjoying each other's company.

Jean used to say that we complemented each other. I'd force her to socialize, and she'd slow me down to a more normal pace. It worked well for us.

Oh yes, I still get frustrated with her. It doesn't matter how long we've been together, I can't fully understand the Face Blindness and how she has to cope with it. I don't have it. My brain doesn't work the same way hers does. I've had to accept that fact. To cope with it myself.

If I had to describe Face Blindness, or what I perceive it to be like, I think of it like looking at an abstract painting. You know the kind I'm talking about. Picasso – with the face all in weird blocks, almost unrecognizable. When you look at the painting, it makes no sense. You try to put the structure together. You read the plaque underneath to see what the artist says about the painting. You still don't see it. I think that's as close as I can get to imagining what Face Blindness must be like.

I can see the distinct details and personalities on a person's face. Face Blindness makes the face a cloud or a blank mask. Two eyeballs. A mouth moving. Yet they see nothing. Like there's nobody there. Just like an abstract painting.

For example, Lewis, a fellow writer, came to visit Jean. Jean would know that she was talking to Lewis because she was expecting him and recognized his voice. However, later, when I asked about the visit, Jean would draw a blank of the person. With much thought, she may remember something about the person, but by the next day, the image would be

totally gone. Unless I quizzed her on it. She would play the scene over and over in her mind so that she could come up with something. Anything! If she hadn't written it down, she might have nothing.

To me, not remembering someone's face is a total drainage of what makes you 'you.' A lot of what is found on the face is what makes them an individual: their expressions and how they react to things.

With Jean, she doesn't get any of that. She doesn't see it, doesn't remember it. It is more than a death; it is the total erasure of a person. Like they've never existed in the first place.

Where does that memory go? Why doesn't it stick? That's Face Blindness.

I can't fathom it!

Even with me, I will say, "Look, I got my hair cut today."

Jean would not recognize the difference.

I had grown that mustache without her knowing. She didn't recognize me. She thought I looked like a convict.

I thought, *We've been married twenty-five years, and you can't recognize me because of a mustache?*

I couldn't get my head around it even then.

Jean likes doing community service, giving back to other people. This in itself amazes me knowing what I do now of how difficult she finds it dealing with people in general. She used to visit an elderly woman in a nursing home every week. The woman had been in the nursing home for two years with a stroke. Before that, Jean would visit her at the woman's trailer. Sometimes, Jean would take the children. It was a good way to teach them the value of spending time with the elderly and to show some of the difficulties the elderly face each day. Jean knew what room the woman was in. This particular day, Jean went in as usual and started chatting with the woman in the bed, not realizing it wasn't her lady. But the kids knew right away. The nurses had changed the lady's room, and Jean didn't know.

To me, it was like, *You've been visiting this woman for how long? And you didn't recognize that it was the wrong person?* I didn't realize that Jean can see a person over and over again and still, there is no recognition. She couldn't remember what the elderly lady looked like.

The kids thought it was hilarious. They'd tease their mother relentlessly for years about the incident, not understanding. Kids! Though I must say that they were never judgmental. I think that's because they had grown up with it.

"That's Mom for you," they would say.

I don't know if they ever thought something was off. The kids never said, only that they had a silly mother. There are so many little stories, funny stories. They'd laugh at how she can't remember this person or that person. We would all laugh about it, not to be mean but because it was truly funny. You have to have a sense of humor about it. Otherwise, it was upsetting for Jean. Humor makes it bearable for her.

The longer you're married, the more mutual friends you acquire. We've made many through the years because we've moved around a bit: New York, Texas, back to New York, Illinois, back to New York, Virginia, and then out of the country to New Zealand. With all these moves, we've left friends behind.

Jean saw that elderly lady once a week for years and couldn't recognize her. Can you imagine how hard it would be for her to meet an old friend that she hasn't seen in ages? Impossible!

One time, we met up with friends we hadn't seen in years. I knew who they were right away. I started chatting with them, not noticing that Jean remained silent beside me, offering very little to the conversation.

I kept thinking, *What's wrong with her? Why doesn't she jump in and say something?* not realizing her inner struggle.

Afterward, when we walked away, she was real quiet. It suddenly hit me; she didn't know who they were.

I remember another time (this one is more recent) when we had decided to take our pug, Brutus, for a walk. There's a lake in Hamilton. It's a beautiful walk, about two miles around. The lake is surrounded by homes overlooking the water. We parked at Innes Commons, one of the large public parks that surround the lake, and started our walk from there. As we rounded a corner, we both noticed some new homes being built. Construction workers in high visibility vests and safety helmets were working around the site.

"Uwe!" one of the men called out.

Jean and I stopped as a young man came over to the fence. It was Viv, our youngest son's best friend. We stood chatting for a few minutes. All the while, Jean remained silent by my side. After we said goodbye and started on our way again, Jean leaned in and whispered,

"Who was that?"

I looked at her in shock. "Really? That's Viv!"

"No. Really? That guy was Viv?"

She turned around and studied Viv who had gone back to work.

"It must be the work clothes," she muttered as an excuse.

I shook my head. We've known Viv since we've been in New Zealand. He'd come over to the house regularly before both boys got married and life took over.

You see what I'm getting at? It happens all the time. It must be so frustrating for Jean.

Knowing what I know now and looking back, I should have been more aware of her, for example, when Jean would get a haircut or do something special and I wouldn't say anything or even notice. I didn't understand what it really meant to her.

I should have been the one to say, "Oh, I see you did this or that," because, for Jean, it means something more than normal. It is something that we take for granted. But for her, it meant that it made her an individual, which she instinctively was craving, despite not knowing why that feeling was lacking.

It's more than just feeling good about oneself. I don't think she does this intentionally. It goes deeper for Jean than just noticing the change in her. Since she can't remember distinctions about other people, it would be nice for others to remember things about her, to notice the changes. To give her peace of mind that she is unique, a distinct person, and not some abstract face.

It's human nature to want to belong. For Jean, this seems like an impossible dream.

People can't see Face Blindness. It's not like being in a wheelchair where others are aware of the limitations of the person. I've seen the expressions on people's faces when Jean tells them about the Face Blindness and that she doesn't remember them. It's almost anger.

"We're supposed to be friends, and you don't remember me?"

It goes right back onto Jean, and it's not fair. It shouldn't be that way at all. I feel for her. People speak down to her. It happens many times.

This is my perspective on it: Jean grew up with Face Blindness, not knowing it as a kid, thinking that people don't like her. "I'd rather be by myself." It's all part of it. It's the facet of being afraid that if you tell someone that you won't remember them that they aren't going to want to be with you. They're not going to want you.

Rejection.

What young person doesn't want friends? So, you're going to hide it. You're going to do what you can do to live with it, though not knowing what 'it' is.

It's the same now in Jean's adulthood. Why does she have to put all the effort in? It should be both persons. And they should understand her limitations and work with them.

Nine:

# Relationships

*"I am what I am, an' I'm not ashamed. 'Never be ashamed,' my ol' dad used ter say, 'there's some who'll hold it against you, but they're not worth botherin' with.'"*

*Rubeus Hagrid in* Harry Potter and the Goblet of Fire
*by JK Rowling*

The way I am is the way I am. I've accepted that fact. It is what it is. I don't look upon Face Blindness as a handicap. However, the way society is structured makes it difficult not to, especially when it comes to building relationships.

Imagine someone in a wheelchair, say a paraplegic. You don't expect that person to get up and walk. You're not offended that they can't. Society has done things to help them: ramps are made, accessible parking spots are provided, bathrooms are built to accommodate the wheelchair… It's a visible problem and easily understood.

I, too, have a problem. Yet very few people attempt to understand it or believe that it is a real thing. Because it's not visible, most dismiss it. No matter how hard I try, I cannot live up to their expectations. Just like the paraplegic, there are things I physically cannot do.

People think I'm rude, or haughty, or stuck up – *She thinks she's better than us,* kind of thing. I've heard it with my own ears. And this comes from people who supposedly know me.

I'm not doing it on purpose. It's similar to people with Tourette syndrome, except that is very overt. Face Blindness is covert and thus insidious. You look normal. You behave normally. You look like you're social in social settings. Yet you are far from feeling normal.

When I realized I had an issue, I did try hard to figure out who was who but soon gave up.

The constant trying and failing made my stress levels go through the roof. It became apparent very quickly that the exercise was futile. So I gave up and felt better for it. Not defeated. Relieved. You can't live life stressed out the entire time.

I don't have a wheelchair to let people know that I have a handicap. It's hard getting over the hump of "Oh, I can't remember people too." It's not the same. For me, it's more complicated than that.

For some, they just don't get it. Others will ask questions.

You quickly get a sense of who cares and who doesn't. Who really wants to know and who can't be bothered.

Face Blindness makes you self-contained because you end up living in a bubble. The bubble is that day. Only that day. It's about how you are functioning in that day, independent of the past, whether it was yesterday, a week ago, a month, or a year. None of that matters. Just that day.

Keeping that in mind, you can see why being social is very difficult. It doesn't matter if I'm with the same group of people two to three times a week. It's like walking in for the first time each time, even though I know that I know these people. I may recognize someone who had spent quality time with me, but that is also a fickle beast and tends to come and go with no rhyme or reason. Names are not remembered, or very rarely.

To combat this, I've recently become more vocal about my Face Blindness. I will ask my friends when they come up to me to say their name and what we did last together, or the last conversation we had had. I call this a trigger or a prompt. It will help me recall what we did together – but not the face. Never the face.

I generally like people. I try hard to be social. I love sharing facts, sharing life experiences, and just plain feeling like I belong. How do I manage this socialization?

Since my brain cannot use facial recognition, it has to draw information from other sources. When I was younger, it was doing this automatically. Only as an adult and after I realized I had Face Blindness have I become aware of what I was doing.

I read people, analyzing them: the way they approach me, their body language, facial expressions, and tone of voice. These give me clues about whether I know this person, how I know this person, how they are feeling, and how it links or doesn't link to me. It gives me a framework to build on, all done in a matter of seconds. It's an automatic function, often carried out subconsciously. Add in the person's voice and speech pattern, and I have enough information to work with.

I ask myself, "How do I know this person? Where do they fit into my life?" and go from there.

I also have tried and trusted tricks to help me. I keep a repertoire of 'topics for discussion' to be used in social settings. All are neutral subjects. I learned to ask questions, to draw the other person out. This serves two purposes: 1) to help put this person in a category: family, friend, acquaintance, etc., and 2) to disguise my problem.

For example, when working in a dental practice, one of my duties was to bring the patient back to the treatment room and make the patient comfortable. Anybody who's been to the dentist knows that it's hard to relax in the chair. So, I would talk about this and that to try to take their mind off the procedure to come, putting them at some degree at ease. I became good at this 'small talk,' and the patients loved it. Now, I apply this technique in all settings. It helps keep me from looking stupid. The small talk also helps me fish out information that I can use to trigger a memory or figure out where the person fits on my scale of 'people I should know and remember, or not.'

What if someone is in a bad mood? For me, anything out of the ordinary changes everything: their looks, their voice, even their posture. This can make things much harder for me.

As usual, I first have to figure out how I know them. The next question is, *Are they in a bad mood because of me?* One of my coping mechanisms is that I always give people the benefit of the doubt, because I don't have the information needed to base any assumptions on. I will make excuses for their feelings, such as that they are having a bad day, or are sick, or something went wrong. I make the assumption that their mood is never associated with me and that I am not the problem. This system has worked for me, and I still use it.

As far as altercations go, I'm not an aggressive person by nature. I like to fix things and tend to be the peacemaker. I really don't like making waves. I think it's a subconscious measure to protect myself.

And yes, altercations do happen. That is a part of life. But I have a unique advantage because of the Face Blindness. I don't carry around emotional baggage, such as holding a grudge, carrying resentment, or being jealous, envious, or even depressed.

Why not?

Because emotional baggage is usually attached to people and the complications that come with them. I can't remember people. Thus, I can't remember the emotion tied to them. Forgiveness is easy because I quickly forget. This is one of the few blessings of having Face Blindness.

Though I may not recognize a face, I do instinctively recognize when to be wary of someone, even if I don't have the exact memory as to why. Like anybody else, I want to protect myself, cocoon my feelings. Time may go by, but my brain will retain certain facts. I call it a gut feeling, but the logical part of me knows that my brain has enough information to trigger warning signals for me to be cautious. In this instance, I don't need a face. My brain has learned to figure it out without one.

I'm a real huggy person. I don't know why. Maybe it's my way of connecting with people through physical contact where I feel I'm lacking that connection. A sense of being human.

Or maybe it's a default thing to try to show that I have some feelings towards other people, even though I don't.

Or maybe I use it to place people in a category – family, friend, or stranger. I'll hug perfect strangers on the chance that I might actually know them. If they're coming in for a hug, you know I'm going to give one back. Are they going to give me a kiss too? Well, okay.

Do people misinterpret that sometimes? Probably. But it's too late. The hug's over.

You might wonder if guys will think I am coming onto them? I don't think so, but how can I know for sure? I avoid looking at people, so it's easy to miss any signals. It never enters my mind anyway. I am self-contained. What others think, do, or say has little effect on me.

My friend Lewis asked this question of me on one of our trips to a writers' meeting – if guys think I'm coming onto them by my freely hugging them. It took me aback. Like I said, it had never entered my mind, so I didn't know how to answer. But it got me thinking and made me re-evaluate my actions. If hugging gave the wrong signals to men, I didn't want that. Since that conversation, I haven't been as free with my hugs. I find that sad, especially when it's one of the few ways I can connect with people and feel somewhat normal.

There are funny moments, though, moments that are harmless but embarrassing: times when Face Blindness had me talking to strangers who I thought were someone else.

I've been caught out so many times in the grocery store when I was first married. Uwe and I used to do our weekly food shopping together. I liked to compare costs and ingredients.

One time, I was studying a can of baked beans.

I turned to the man standing next to me and asked, "Hey, babe, what do you think of this brand?"

I held out the can and then, looked up to find some random man. He looked sheepishly at me, and then I knew. He wasn't Uwe.

"That's a mighty fine can of baked beans," the man said with a smile, "but I'm not your babe."

I cringed and smiled back at him, embarrassed, and said,

"Oh, I'm sorry. I thought you were my husband." I slinked away with my cart and the beans. I didn't care about the beans anymore, if they were right or wrong. I just wanted to get out of there.

This wasn't the first incident. Spaghetti. Cereal. Butter. You pick an aisle, any aisle, and I'd be there talking to strange men. My poor husband. He must have thought me a looney. It happened all the time, way before I even knew I had Face Blindness. I felt like such an idiot.

Another example was when I was shopping with my teenage daughter, Leia. She wanted a new bathing suit for our trip to Orlando, Florida. I don't know if you've had a teenager or not… but they can be difficult at times. This was one of them. She wanted a string bikini, which was the rage at the time. Being a mother, I wanted more coverage than a couple patches of material held together by strings. I found a two-piece suit I thought was a good compromise and went to find her. (She is a good shopper with an eye for the bargain, so back then, she was always disappearing looking for the next great find.)

I found a dark-haired girl looking at the sales rack. So naturally, I thought it was her.

"Hey," I said, holding up the bathing suit. "What about this one? It's a two-piece like you want and in the color you like."

The girl turned around to see who was talking and gave me one of those looks. You know the kind: the ones that say, 'Are you crazy, lady?' Maybe I am, but I couldn't say that out loud.

Obviously, it wasn't my daughter. I realized that fairly quickly.

"Oh, sorry. I thought you were my daughter," I said, and walked away.

I still needed to find my daughter, which I eventually did.

And yes, she did like the bathing suit, so we both went home happy. I didn't tell her about my mistake in the store. Believe me, my children had enough ammunition on me already, and boy, did they love to use it. Kids!

That's just two examples. There are so many. Humiliations galore. I find them hilarious now. My family has a good laugh with me when we talk about those incidents. Humor is the best antidote. I love it.

~

In general, I pay very little attention to people, to their faces. I know there is no point. It makes me oblivious to the signals of interest a man might send me. That was one of the issues I had in high school. I thought nobody liked me, and when you're a teenage girl, for guys to like you is critical to your sense of self-worth.

It wasn't until my fifteen-year class reunion, when we were all joking about those awkward years, that the guys admitted, "Ah, we really liked you! We wanted to ask you out, but we were stupid."

Dan was the only one who tried, and I didn't remember that until I read his interview. So, obviously, I didn't pick up on the signals that the guys must have been throwing my way.

It's the same today.

I don't see the signals and thus am ignorant of any attempts by the opposite sex to get my attention. But if you saw my husband, you would know that a glare from him would be as good a deterrent as a can of skunk oil.

Besides, I'm interested in platonic relationships. My hug hopefully reflects that. No one has said otherwise. Should I start asking?

~

Most memories are based around people.

For me however, the people are not important. My brain

has learned not to dwell on them because it's pointless. My brain lacks the ability to recall that information though it is stored in my frontal lobe. I can only recall the event.

So, where is the emotion of the memory, of the relationship? Where do I place this ghost figure in the hierarchy of relationships? People to avoid versus people to keep around. What do they give me? Friendship? Comfort? Trouble? Hurt?

When you think of shared experiences, the memory leaves behind a reference as to how you're going to deal with that person if/when you meet again – where they fit in, what level of intimacy they share with you. I don't have that.

So, what does that leave me with?

Not much.

## Ten:

# Friendships

Shrek: *Why… are you following me?*
Donkey: *Oh, I'll tell you why. [sings]*
*'Cause I'm all alone.*
*There's no one here beside me.*
*My problems have all gone.*
*There's no one to deride me!*
*But ya gotta have friends!*
Shrek: *Stop singing! Well, it's no wonder you don't have any*
*friends.*
Donkey: *Wow! Only a true friend would be that truly honest.*

Shrek *– screenplay by Ted Elliott and others*

The teenage arena had long been left behind me. Adulthood was well established. A husband. Children. Home. A routine of life. A rhythm.

Maintaining friendships remained a problem during this time; not that it really bothered me. I was used to being alone. Uwe was enough for me. That's what I kept telling myself.

Some help would come later in an unexpected form – social media – a but that was still a distant dream. Even cellphones would eventually help by providing instant communication through phone calls and texting. Again, they were only just becoming available in the mid-80s. The technology consisted of those clunky plastic bricks attached to a huge battery and was way too expensive. Only the sophisticated businessman and the construction boss-type people carried them around. They looked so cool back then. We laugh now. No one would be caught dead with one of those monstrosities these days.

Until my mid-thirties, friendships were still made the old-fashion way. You meet. You mingle. You slowly get to know each other. You decide you like the person. You make arrangements to get together again. That was the usual process back before cellphones and social media became the new normal.

It could be meeting someone at the park with the children, or the library, or some other event. It could be meeting someone at music lessons, a work-do, sitting at the botanical gardens writing on your laptop.

People are everywhere. It only takes someone to express an interest in you, or to have something in common with you, and the friendship could start.

I see this process happen all around me: the outsider looking into the snow-globe of other people's lives. Observing people is a pastime of mine. It helps with creating believable characters when it comes to writing. It also helps me feel like I'm a part of something, even if it's only in the audience watching others' lives unfold.

I'm not saying that this process of friendship doesn't happen to me. I know it has.

A person approaches. I see them smile. It is tentative. Someone who doesn't know me. I know this in the way they hold their body, their head, the distance they set themselves apart from me.

All this takes a brief second for my brain to absorb. Simultaneously, my stress levels go up.

*What will I say? Should I tell them that I have a problem remembering people? Will I remember them the next time? I need an anchor point. Look for some fact that I can implant in my brain.*

That's what goes through my head as someone comes towards me: I search for a plan of attack, as if facing a difficult challenge, not a person. It's as though I have already distanced myself from the other person by making it mechanical instead of personal. This process is automatic. A survival tactic. All the while, I would be smiling as if I'm a 'normal' person.

Inside, I'm crying, "I want to remember!"

It is futile. I know it, yet still I keep trying. I wouldn't be human if I didn't.

Uwe, my husband, was my friend, the one constant person in my life. I was satisfied with that – having one friend. However, he still didn't understand my condition and felt I should branch out and try to make other friends. He was very social and thrived around people. I was happy by myself. It was easier.

In any marriage, you try to please your partner. So, I made an effort to make friends. Moving as often as we did, made it more difficult for me. Each move was a huge obstacle. Starting over again with new people and the stress of trying to figure out who was who. Uwe had no problem. For me, it was torture.

Uwe made sure we met people right away, whether it was at church or work based. Uwe made friends first. We'd be invited to their house or Uwe would ask them to ours. We usually ended up playing board games or cards, or the guys would be watching sports while we women talked.

When the children came along, we gravitated to those who had similarly aged children. Though I didn't pick these people out, I was happy with this arrangement. Uwe carried the load of the friendships. I kept up an appearance. Not that I didn't try. I did. But it took so much energy. It was easier to be a bystander, to pretend to be a part of the group, than to be intimately involved in a friendship.

Then, it happened. The unexpected. I experienced an instant connection with another person. I'm not talking about love at first sight. This was deeper. A kindred spirit, a connection that touched the inner soul. Undeniable. Inescapable. A binding of two people that has no explanation.

Maybe this is normal. I don't know. It's not for me.

The first time it happened, it was like a lightning bolt had struck me. I had an instant awareness of something special.

We had moved south to Hampton, Virginia, for Uwe's job. We didn't know anyone. Being the social one, my husband got to work right away making new friends, whereas I was more reluctant than usual. I don't know why. Maybe it was the stress of the move or facing a new culture – the southern way – or I was just tired of more new faces.

Then I met Cindy, at church. I walked in and felt it before I even saw her. That connection. I was drawn to Cindy like iron to a magnet. We hit it off right away. It didn't matter what she looked like. She was smart, sophisticated, athletic, and artistic. The pull between us was undeniable.

Is this what it felt like to have a friend? No wonder people strive for it! It was the most amazing feeling I had ever felt – this connection with another human being. I thought I had it with my husband, but this was something different, something on a cellular level.

Our friendship was intense. Talking to Cindy was easy. We felt the same about many things. Our intellects were equal, and our conversations reflected that. I may not be good with people, but I am not a dumb person. My head is full of (what I hope are) interesting facts. I can reason and follow logic with the best of them. It also helped that our sons were of the same age and liked to hang out together.

I finally had a friend – a real friend.

I was in heaven. I was so happy. I felt human. I felt like I finally was normal. Each time Cindy and I met, I came alive again. It became a drug, and I wanted more of it: of that affirmation.

Like most good things, it came to a sudden end. I really don't know what happened. One day we were friends. The next day, I was ignored, shunned, cast off like last year's fashion. No words of explanation were given. She just turned her back on me, and that was it.

I was more than hurt. I was devastated. For the first time, I had felt what it was like to have a proper friend. To have a deep connection with another human being. And then, it was gone, taken away in an instant.

This is what death must feel like. That loss. The deep pit of despair.

And yet, there she was each time I went to church or social functions, alive and breathing, talking to others and ignoring me. It was as if I didn't exist anymore, which was a worse kind of death.

Why didn't I ask her what happened? I don't know. I think I was in shock. Then denial. It hurt so much. I felt betrayed, a stabbing to the heart.

I said to Uwe, "Never again. It's not worth it!"

That was the anger in me. It lasted a long time until, finally, I let her go, mourning the loss of what was and what could have been.

Years later, I met Cindy again. That connection was still there. I could feel it. I wanted it. Needed it. I so wanted to ask her what had happened to turn her away from me, to fix whatever wrong I had done. But I didn't. Too much time had gone by. Our lives went on different paths. Our conversations should have been natural, and they were at first. But the more we talked, the more it felt like a competition as if Cindy was trying to top whatever I had been doing. It confirmed what I already knew: what we had had was, indeed, over.

Only recently I learned that there had been a disagreement between our two sons and that was what ended our friendship. How petty. Such a small thing. They were teenagers. Cindy was an adult. She should have talked to me about it. I guess it truly wasn't a real friendship after all. That hurt even more.

After Cindy, I was afraid to reach out. It took a special couple to make me feel at ease again. Uwe and I met Todd and Verna through mutual friends. They are such an odd couple. Verna is all sophistication, and Todd is as country as one can get. Total opposites. They have been our constant friends over the past twenty years, even after we moved out of the country. Something about them sticks with me. I can remember their voices as soon as I hear them. Verna has a unique southern accent and a particular way she uses tonal inflections in her speech. As soon as she speaks, I know it's her. Todd, too, has a certain way about him when he talks. He approaches his speech as if he has a great story to tell you, which he usually does. I also recognize Todd by his posture when he talks and the way he uses gestures. And his hilarious stories.

These two special people stay in my mind. I may forget about them for a bit, but it doesn't take much of a prompt to bring them back into my head. That is a great feat and is accomplished by only a few people in my life. They don't know how much I treasure them.

~

We faced another cultural shift when we moved to New Zealand. Making friends was at the top of our list, especially for our two teenage children that moved with us. Our oldest son stayed back in Virginia. Uwe had been in New Zealand for two months before I arrived with the children. During that time, he had been busy making connections.

That first weekend, we went over to some folks' home for a barbecue. Another family was there with their teenage son, Lincoln, who was the same age as our son, Lane. However, Lincoln wasn't the only one who came. His older brother, Ben, was also present along with his sister, Suzanna.

Something unexpected happened. That instant connection! The same feeling that I had experienced with Cindy. I recognized it right away. To my alarm, it was with Ben who was in his early twenties.

I was floored! It was so unexpected. What was I to do about that? He was a young man, and I felt that kindred spirit with him. I could tell that he felt it too.

Don't get the wrong idea. There was nothing sexual about it. Just like with Cindy, this was purely on a friendship level, a meeting of intellect, a oneness of mind and spirit.

At first, I tried to ignore the call of the connection. We were new in the country. We didn't know the culture. I didn't know who these people were. They didn't know us. However, that kindred spirit is a powerful force and difficult to deny, especially for someone like me with Face Blindness who really struggles with friendships.

I reasoned, *How can I deny myself this connection with another human being? It's not fair that others fall into friendships so easily where I have to struggle just to fit in. I deserve a friend!*

Male or female. It didn't matter to me. It was the connection I craved. The joy of remembering someone for more than a brief interlude of time.

Uwe and I bought a house in a small town called Te Awamutu, situated twenty minutes from Hamilton where Uwe and I both worked. Lane and Lincoln became friends. Lincoln lived in Hamilton, which meant that I was driving Lane to the city on a regular basis.

Through Lincoln, Lane met more young people his age

and expanded his circle of friends. Ben was a part of that group, more because he was interested in one of the girls than anything else. We were thrown into the same circle and soon gravitated to each other.

What would a woman my age have in common with a young man? But it wasn't about what we had in common or not. It was about the oneness of spirit. It's hard to explain unless you've experienced it.

Soon, we were texting, sparring with words. It became a game of intellect: who could outsmart the other. We were equally matched, which made it even more fun. When we were together whether at parties, playing pool or touch rugby (yes, I played rugby), we would gravitate towards each other. Just talking. Our topics of conversation were mostly on books that we had read or not read. Ben was a great reader. So was I. It was a topic I never tired of discussing.

Ben rarely talked about the girl he liked, Cayley. It was obvious to all, even to Cayley, that he was into her. When he did finally ask for advice, I was there to help. And when Cayley hurt him, I was there to pick him up.

"There will be someone else," I said to him. "Someone who will appreciate you for who you are. You need to wait for that person."

All the while, I was aware of how our friendship looked. Though it was strictly platonic, it could have been misconstrued by our easy nature when we were in company. As happens, it was.

For most of my outings with Lane, meeting his friends for a game of pool, or for rugby or whatever, Uwe very rarely came along. We thought he wasn't interested. Since the move to New Zealand, he had grown moody and depressed. I thought it was the strain of moving to a new country, the new culture, and job. But it was something more secretive.

The signs had been there back in Virginia when he had had a nervous breakdown. However, I still didn't know what I was looking at. Two years had passed, and Uwe was a changed person. We were only beginning to investigate his health. I knew there was something wrong even though he kept denying it.

Then came the issue of my friendship with Ben. It wasn't like Ben was the only person I was hanging out with. I had made friends with Cayley and her two sisters. This put me in close association with their mother, Jillian.

I liked the girls. They were fun and full of youthful energy. I was at their house a lot with Lane and got to spend some time with Jillian.

I thought, "Here is a woman I'd like to get to know better."

The family was initially from South Africa. Mementos of their former life decorated their house: tall giraffes carved out of wood, wooden furniture, African keepsakes on tables and walls, the safari color scheme. I found their life interesting, so I made an effort to be Jillian's friend. This wasn't an easy thing for me to do. Unlike with Ben and Cindy, I had only her voice for recognition.

I still didn't talk much about the Face Blindness. Most people just brushed it off with the saying, "I'm terrible with names and faces too."

I didn't press the issue. I probably should have. It was hard because we were Americans in a 'Kiwi' society. We had our funny American ways and sayings. They teased us about them, all in good humor, just as we teased them back. However, internally, I was afraid to be open about the Face Blindness thing, afraid they would tease me about it. I know they would have thought it harmless fun, but for me, I couldn't risk the hurt. No matter what I did to protect myself, it tended to backfire.

I'll give you an example. The lunch break at the dental

clinic I worked at was an hour long. Sometimes I would read in the tiny break room. Other times I would go for a walk or go out for sushi. One of my favorite sushi shops was a few blocks away in a hidden walkway, between two streets, called Casabella Lane. All the locals knew of the lane. Boutique shops lined both sides. They were unique, a real treat for the shopper. The sushi shop was found at the center of the lane where it opened up into a courtyard of Italian fountains and trimmed hedges. A French cafe along with a vegetarian shop was on one side. The other side was my sushi shop and a florist.

On one of my walks, I was passing through the courtyard and a voice called out. It was Jillian. She was sitting outside the French restaurant having lunch with a woman.

As you do, you say your greetings. I turned to the woman.

"Hi, I'm Jean," I said to her.

"Hi," the woman said.

We stared at each other in a moment of awkwardness.

"Have we met before?" That's what I should have asked. Instead, I went with, "What was your name?"

Jillian spoke up and said, "You don't know who this is?"

Oh, boy. Now I was stuck.

"No." And then, I asked, "Have we met before?"

"This is Mary." (I'm picking out a random name. I can't remember the one Jillian used.)

I reached my hand out. 'Mary' tentatively took it. We shook hands.

"Nice to meet you," I said.

The woman looked at me with confusion, and something else I didn't recognize.

Jillian burst out laughing, "You're kidding. Right? This is Sue! You've talked to her before. You've taken her girls to my house."

I was mortified. I honestly didn't know this woman,

didn't recognize her voice. Later, I learned that Sue had taken offense that I hadn't remembered her. I didn't realize that she suffered from depression and already had friendship issues. Not knowing her name had made her feel insignificant, that she didn't matter to me.

As soon as I found out, I apologized. I tried to explain to Sue why I didn't recognize her that day in Casabella Lane – that it had nothing to do with her at all. It was all me. I'm not sure she understood. Most people don't.

After that, I said to myself, "It's not worth it. I am going to tell everyone I meet that I have Face Blindness and that I won't remember them. Then the burden isn't all mine."

Needless to say, my friendship with Jillian didn't last. I was spending too much time with her daughters, taking them here and there because I had the car, and I was trying to keep Lane happy with his friends. Her youngest daughter and Lane had formed an attachment. Then, it went sour. I think this was part of the problem. Whatever the case, Jillian abruptly ended our friendship. Accusations were made. Hurtful words were said, mostly behind my back. I can't remember what, and it doesn't really matter. At the time, I was shunned. Years of trying to be friends with this family were wasted. What was the point of it all?

In a way, I was relieved our friendship was over. I'd tried hard with Jillian, and it didn't work.

"Never again," I said later to Uwe.

"You can't give up just because of one person," he said.

"They don't understand how hard it is for me. It's not worth it. It's too hard. I'm happy to be alone."

And secretly, I still had Ben.

~

Gas prices had risen. We were paying two hundred dollars a week to make the commute back and forth between Te Awamutu and Hamilton. The time had come to move closer to work. That meant living in Hamilton, which brought Lane closer to his friends and me in easier contact with Ben.

Uwe's jealousy escalated. Not that we had done anything wrong. We were always in public and with other people. I can't really blame Uwe. How could Uwe understand when we, as husband and wife, didn't share the same depth of connection as I had had with Cindy and now had with Ben?

The timing was terrible, I must admit. Uwe had been diagnosed with Grave's disease, yet he refused to believe it. His paranoia was in full swing. There was no reasoning with him. The disease was causing a chemical imbalance in his brain, which played havoc with his mental abilities. He became Jekyll and Hyde. It was a terrible time for us. It got to a point where I gave Uwe an ultimatum.

"Go get help or I am leaving you! No waiting. No excuses. You go to the doctor tomorrow and get help. Not next week. Not in two days. Tomorrow!"

I meant it. I was at my wit's end. Poor Lane was stuck in the middle, seeing the mental deterioration of his father first-hand. I couldn't take anymore, for Lane, for me, or for Uwe. I stilled cared about my husband though he couldn't see it. Otherwise, why would I have stayed and put up with his behavior?

No matter how I tried to explain that Ben's friendship was purely platonic, Uwe was convinced that we were having an affair.

"Me? You don't know me at all, do you?" I said, growing angry.

"I don't believe you," was his reply.

"Everyone knows that Ben has feelings for Cayley. It's common knowledge. Ask anyone!"

"I know you cheated!"

"Fine! If that's what you believe, that we are having an affair, then go confront Ben," I demanded.

Uwe did and found out just what I had said: nothing was going on. I felt so sorry for Ben, putting him in that position. After that, we curbed our communications. Yet, it was hard to deny that kindred connection. I still wanted it, wanted that close friendship with Ben.

At that point, when Uwe was at his worst, I considered leaving him just for some peace. Not with Ben, of course. That was never a consideration. However, we both knew that our friendship couldn't go on. I was a married woman. We both knew the friendship looked odd.

Soon after this point, Cayley was in a serious relationship with Lane's best friend, Viv. Ben was upset. I can't blame him. She did lead him on for a while. Ben took a job in Germany, about as far as he could go to get away from New Zealand. Sometimes I wonder if he took it to get away from me, too. To break clean from what became an awkward friendship. Maybe it was a good thing. I don't know.

Like Cindy, it hurt. Not that he had left. I understood his need to get away and had accepted it. What hurt was the emptiness it left behind, the loss of a kindred connection.

Since then, Ben has found a lovely woman and married her. They live in Holland. Once in a while, Ben and I catch up, through email or when he comes back home for a visit. We pick up where we left off, as if no time has gone by. But those times have become less and less common as the years roll by.

~

Face Blindness has its good points and its bad points.

The good point is that I lose the memory of any hurt or pain caused by a person or people. If not a total loss, then at least a dullness of that memory, like peering at it through a fog. Oh, I may retain a sense of caution. Such as when I meet Jillian every so often, I don't remember the specific events leading to our breakup. However, I do feel a need to be wary around her. It's a gut instinct.

We all experience those terrible moments with people – sometimes long drawn out emotional dramas, sometimes just awkward moments that you want to forget. I have that ability to forget. It's not a choice. I look at it as a blessing. It's my superpower. Without all that negative baggage, I am generally a happy person, and that's a great thing!

On the other hand, it makes me feel alone. Without those memories of friends, good and bad, there is nothing. Just me. Fortunately, I like myself now. It makes the loneliness bearable.

It's not that I don't have friends. I do. I just can't remember who they are.

Now, I am vocal about my disorder.

If I'm unsure, I will say, "I have Face Blindness and don't remember people. Have we met before?"

Or, if I know they are new, I will say, "Hi, I'm Jean Gilbert. I have Face Blindness and will not remember you. If you keep talking, I will learn your voice."

Later, after the conversation, or if I know we will meet again, I will say, "The next time we meet, please tell me your name again and what we talked about or where we were. This will help place you in my mind and give me an anchor point. The more you talk to me, the better the chances are that I will recognize you by your voice."

For example, Lewis is my friend, a writer like me. I know he's my friend because each time we meet he tells me his name and gives me an anchor point. We have a shared history. I can tell by his persona and body language. Plus, Lewis has a very distinct tattoo on his arm, a visible marking that I remember. I recognize his voice, too.

It's not the importance of remembering the specific things we have done together, but more that I can sense that we have shared experiences. That's what is important to me.

That's what tells me you are my friend. The more time I spend with you, the higher the chance that I will retain those memories for longer.

All that being said, I no longer hide my problem. I have hurt people by my silence. I've created too many awkward situations that were unnecessary. Yes, some are funny. Some make good stories, which my children love to tease me with. But mostly, they're hurtful. I don't normally share this part. Who would understand?

I haven't entirely given up on friendship, though I don't think I will ever have another link like I did with Cindy and Ben. Two in a lifetime is more than anyone can ask for. I feel really lucky.

What I do ask for is your help. I can't do it on my own.

I'm not like other people. It takes more work on your part to be my friend, for me to remember that you are my friend.

Please, make the effort - for me. It will be worth it, I promise.

Eleven:

# The Closest Friend – Uwe

*"A friend is one that knows you as you are, understands where you have been, accepts what you have become, and still, gently allows you to grow."*

*Anon*

I can understand why Jean feels she can live without people. It must be hard work trying to figure out who's who and where they fit into her life. I feel for her. Jean thinks that she doesn't have close friends because people see her as snobbish, aloof, and just not interested in them. But it's not her fault because she honestly can't remember them. Now Jean is at the point in her life where she tells people outright about her brain disorder.

Jean will say something like this:

"I have a brain problem. It's called Face Blindness. I will not remember you. Please, tell me your name. Tell me what we did together. Tell me what I laughed at, what we shared."

For those who do this, it helps to place them somewhere that Jean can use. She'll put it together.

This only works if people will do it for her. But most don't. They don't understand. Or they think Jean is joking. Jean will ask again and again for people to help her remember them. I've been there and heard her. When they don't, she doesn't recall them.

People come back to her and say, "I said hello to you on the street, and you didn't even say anything. What did I do to you?"

It crushes Jean every time. She tries to hide it, but I see it, and it hurts me too. It hurts that she loses friendships because of it. I can't imagine how she must feel. This is why she tells me that it's easier not to have friends, to be alone than to get hurt continually. She deserves better. Jean is a great person if they only tried to understand and work around the Face Blindness.

Jean is quite good at covering up her problem. She has always been prudent when it comes to her interactions with people. It has helped but not totally alleviated the difficulties that arise with relationships. It is more about misunderstandings. Let me explain:

Jean and I have had a pretty good relationship, especially being married so young. At times when we were first married, I would think that she was a bit self-centered or selfish that she wouldn't remember my friends. There were times when I would get a little upset and think that Jean really didn't care about them. I put it down to the kind of person she was – not outgoing, but shy. That was one of her traits. I also put it down to her memory.

When we'd interact with people, I was always telling her who this person was, who that person was, as long as I can remember. For her, there were times when she used to cry and tell me that she just couldn't make friends. Or she'd try and people didn't want to be friends with her. Again, it was because she wasn't able to connect with someone or have deep feelings about someone because she couldn't remember them. It put a lot of people off.

A couple of girls would come to the house.

"Hey, we want to spend time with you. Let's hang out

together," they'd say.

It was Jean's demeanor that was misunderstood. It's not that Jean said anything like, "I don't want to hang out with you." But that's the impression the girls got.

They didn't know that Jean was trying to place in her mind: *Who are these people? How do I know them? Did we do anything together before? And if so, what was it?*

I didn't even know she was doing that.

It upset Jean that the girls didn't want her as a friend. After a while, Jean gave up. For some years, Jean didn't want anyone. I would try to get people to be friends with her, but she was put off by it. At the time, I didn't understand why. She would be a bit cold because of that fact, that worry that 'I will get hurt.'

It's a vicious circle: you find it difficult but you make an effort to make a friend. Just one. You fail. The next time you make an effort, that failure is hanging over you, so you hold back a bit. That makes the friendship more awkward and more likely to fail again. Thus, the circle of effects compounds with each try.

All this was happening before we knew that Jean had Face Blindness.

Now, after years of frustration, Jean has made an effort to tell people about what she needs. A few have tried to work with her. But for the most part, people don't. They think she is telling a story. Jean is resigned to that fact. There's nothing she can do about that. She can't *make* people understand. She's not a person who is going to put herself out there and say, "Can I have a picture of you so that I can write your name and information on it for my records?"

She's not ready to go on a crusade. Can you imagine how much effort and energy it would take to gather that much information about people? It would be exhausting.

Jean tries to be the best friend she can be. But you need to understand what her limitations are. And within those limitations, she tries extremely hard, going beyond the call of duty.

You look at our daughter, Leia, and say, "Man, she looks a lot like Jean." Jean doesn't see it at all. You look at our granddaughter and say, "Man, you can see Lane in her." Jean cannot see it, even if the two pictures are side-by-side, because her brain cannot formulate the connection. What degree Jean suffers, I don't know.

It's only in the last few years, since her brother has been in a Face Blindness study with a Canadian medical research facility, that Jean's come to the conclusion that if she doesn't say anything, she's not going to have friends. She has to let them know. Whereas before she'd tell me, "Oh well. It's pointless. If they can't be bothered, I can't be bothered, either."

For us who don't have Face Blindness, it's hard to understand even when you read about it. Even for me, who lives with it.

I like Jean doing this book because it makes her realize that she's doing okay.

Face Blindness doesn't make her wrong. It doesn't make her less of a person, less of a friend. She is who she is. Jean has to deal with it. People should learn to deal with it too. That's how I look at it. I don't have a problem with it. I accept it for what it is, for who Jean is.

I've always been there for Jean. I never get tired of helping her, saying this is this person, this is what you did with them, at this place. That's what makes us a unit. I have empathy for her. I realize there's nothing I can do to take the problem away from her. It does get her low at times, not having friends. I want to help her.

Once Jean started writing, I used to get upset because she put in so much time and energy into cutting out pictures of

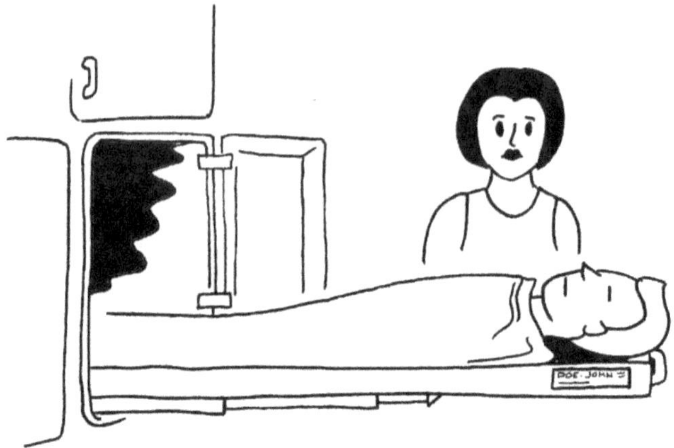



"It's very simple ma'am,
is this your husband or not?"

people and designing characters.

"It's your story! You're already telling it," I'd say.

I didn't understand, and I live with the Face Blindness. I can see why others struggle.

For every single character, Jean writes down everything about them and their personality. The details are to the extreme. To sit there and have to make page after page of information about one character, let alone the rest of them... it blows my mind. You think, *Wow!* and get a better understanding of what she has to go through with real people.

For example, I can remember the characters from The Vault Agency books, one of Jean's science fiction series. I'll pick out two of the main characters – Sharra Lane and Lazarus Maitland – as examples. Just thinking of them, I can easily picture in my mind what they look like, and who they were as people. Jean cannot. That's the thing about it. Jean will go back and read her own work and not 'see' the characters that she has created, even after all the documentation she's put together – that are books in their own right.

Her dedication to her writing takes much more work than the average writer has to do, because of what she has to do to remember.

I'm trying to make the point for people to understand why it is unreasonable to do nothing to help Jean when it comes to friendship. Because of what Jean has to go through to get to know someone, she'd have to do the same thing she does with her characters for each person. Can you imagine what that would be like? How cluttered the house would get? To have a corkboard with details of people pinned to it? Sitting there, studying it, their features, what makes that person an individual, the color of their hair, eyes, skin, etc. For Jean, it would be so difficult, so time-consuming and depressing. No one should ask that of her. It's just not fair.

Jean has to come up with different ways to cope. Sometimes there's a learning curve. For instance, we've moved several times through the years. To a normal person, you realize that you're going to meet new people and make new friends. That's not a problem. For Jean, it's such a big deal because of the process of remembering people. I had to realize that the things I take for granted, for her are obviously a strain. Her problem with people has compounded each time we moved. More people to forget. More people who will have a likelihood of getting upset with her. It's hard to comprehend what that must feel like. It probably would've been best for Jean if we had stayed in one place and grown some roots. But that's said in hindsight. Too late now.

Now, I try to help Jean out by telegraphing information to her without the other person in the conversation knowing what I am doing.

Here's an example from the other day, when I was talking

with my friend, Ron.

"Hey, Ron. (The name.) It was great playing golf with you the other day. (The event.) Jean couldn't stand how much time it took to caddy. (The placement of Jean in the event.)"

If we know we are traveling, there is a lot of coaching before the event.

"This is who we will meet," – and I'll list the important ones.

"This is what we last did with them," – and I'll give Jean the specifics.

"This is some of the things we talked about," – and I'll tell Jean whatever I can remember, usually something relevant to the next event.

It's not like we as a couple are reclusive. Far from it. We meet all kinds of people. Jean, though, needs specific details and where these people fit into our lives.

One thing I've noticed about Jean is that through the years she has concentrated on people's voices even before she knew about the Face Blindness. She'd make comments about them, how the voices stood out to her or were unique in some way. I don't pay attention to voices the same as she does. Now, I understand that she uses voices to recognize people.

Jean will tell you that what drew her to me was my voice. Radio friendly, she'd call it. It's the same with anyone with a distinctive voice. It makes it easier for Jean to recognize the person.

If the voice is difficult for Jean to understand, say with dialect, then that throws another wrench into the cogs of her brain. We'll be watching a show on television, for example, a Scottish detective show called *Shetlands*, and Jean can't understand them at all. I have to continually translate. Sometimes, I even have to keep saying who is who. I wonder if that's all part of it – not understanding the voice/language hinders her recognition of a person. Interesting.

When we moved to New Zealand, it took a few years for Jean to get used to the dialect. I think they all sounded the same to her. That probably didn't help her with making friends either.

It's hard for us to understand what she has to go through. But I expect that Jean would surpass us all when it comes to voice recognition if we were blinded and put to the test. Think about it. That's her primary source of recall, maybe even her only source of recall. I wish others would think about that and give Jean a chance.

Jean needs people to like her.

To love her.

To want to be her friend.

The knowledge of Face Blindness has made a big difference in Jean's life. She has taken it on board like she does everything else in life, with courage and the willpower to tackle it. It comes out in her writing. For years, she has had those stories in her head, but nothing about the individuals and so felt she couldn't do it – be a writer. It was only after she figured out how to manage it with her extensive character books that the courage to write came out. I find this very interesting because it gives us outsiders an idea of what she would have to do with individuals she meets if she wanted to have that person as a close friend. A storyboard for each person or a character book for each friend just to retain that information about them. That, to me, is an astounding fact.

Who of us would be willing to go through that much effort?

We have it so easy.

Twelve:

# Conversation Between Two Friends –

# Lewis and Jean

*"You have been my friend," replied Charlotte. "That in itself is a tremendous thing… after all, what's a life anyway? We're born, we live a little while, we die… By helping you, perhaps I was trying to lift up my life a trifle. Heaven knows anyone's life can stand a little of that."*

*Charlotte in* Charlotte's Web *by E.B. White*

*Jean*: Can you remember the first time we met?

*Lewis*: I remember thinking it was a bit unusual and bizarre.

*Jean*: Bizarre? What did I do that was strange?

*Lewis*: Let me go back. It was 2012. I went to a science fiction convention in Auckland on the recommendation of my friend, Grant. While there, they said to get in touch with the SpecFicNZ group down here in Hamilton, and you were the contact. So, we had organized to meet at the *Strawberry Farm Café*. I remember getting a cryptic email from you to look for someone with auburn hair, a brown laptop satchel, and something else. I think it was what you were wearing. It was weird. It struck me at the time as, *Aah, these writers are just a bunch of freaks.*

*Jean*: Calling me a freak, now. What kind of friend is that?!

*Lewis*: The best kind. Naw, I know now that you're not a freak. In retrospect, you were maybe trying to describe a way in which a person with Face Blindness might recognize someone else. Physical descriptions that would work. But for me, it seemed very unusual. But it didn't worry me because I quite enjoy unusual things happening. So that didn't deter me in the least. Then when you sat down, you turned out fairly normal and studious. Very businesslike. Writing stuff down.

*Jean*: I'm always writing stuff down.

*Lewis*: And direct. Americans are generally a bit more direct compared to New Zealanders. Different kind of manner and demeanor. Generally fairly confident. Might come from being the world's superpower and wasting everyone. That sort of thing. Sort of like Israeli but turned down half-strength. South Africans on quarter speed.

*Jean*: Be nice! Maybe, it's because I'm a New Yorker, and we don't waste time on small talk. We like to get down to business.

*Lewis*: That you do. Kiwis like to chitchat first with business mixed in. A totally different culture.

*Jean*: After that initial meeting, you would come to the SpecificNZ meetings I organized.

*Lewis*: I was farting around with my writing. Too many distractions. You were always on me to get it done. (whipping sounds) I'm getting there. I'm getting there. Anyway, some of our meetings were held in Tauranga. That meant carpooling an hour and a half both ways. Plenty of time to get to know each other. I didn't realize that for you it was like meeting me for the first time for a while.

*Jean*: Before that, we were at the level of passing acquaintances. I was always 'down to business' and not able to retain enough to remember anything about you except that you were a storyteller and that you had a tattoo on your forearm arm.

*Lewis*: You can't remember my face, but you can remember my tattoo.

*Jean*: Weird, huh.

*Lewis*: Interesting.

*Jean*: When did I first tell you about my Face Blindness?

*Lewis*: I think it was on the first or second trip over the Kaimai Range on our way to a SpecFicNZ meeting in Tauranga, or even a farther drive to Papamoa. When you're having just a passing contact with someone, you don't get to find out very much about them. Only what they outwardly portray. I'm quite a chatty person–

*Jean*: Yes, you are.

*Lewis*: I like people and finding out about their background and such, especially someone who's from a different country. It's interesting to find out our different experiences. I'm quite a natural storyteller, and I like telling people interesting stuff that I've done.

*Jean*: I can attest to that. Some, I can't repeat.

*Lewis*: I call them interesting. Okay, bizarre. I've found it's a good way to sift out friends who I don't need. I don't have much censorship in what I say. They can decide whether to be my friend or not. So with you, Jean, you were stuck in the car for long periods of time listening to my stories. That's when you finally shared some things about yourself. Back then, you were a bit cagey about the Face Blindness.

*Jean*: I wasn't yet comfortable telling people about it.

*Lewis*: I can remember one of the first things about Face Blindness you said to me was, "Up until now, I haven't told people about the Face Blindness. Not speaking up has made my life much more difficult. So, I've decided that I'm actually going to tell people about it." And then you went on to explain it. Kind of how it worked. But I think now that you've had practice, it's easier for you to encapsulate it in a two-sentence spiel.

*Jean*: An elevator pitch. Just giving the pertinent information in a nutshell. People can handle only so much.

*Lewis*. Too true. Though you told me about it, I really didn't have the understanding that I have now. I understand that you cannot recognize people. It's kind of a cool thing because you would say, "I'd see you in the street, but I wouldn't be able to recognize who you were." Not cool for you. But for me, that's quite a cool concept of how to understand how it works. Years down the track and helping you with this book, I know that there is more to it than just that. There are different levels, different subtleties, depending on what kind of contact someone has with you and the duration of that contact.

*Jean*: Modern technology helps. When a picture pops up on a text, Facebook, Instagram, or any other site, it really helps me. Compare that to twenty or thirty years ago, I really had nothing. There's a lot more opportunity for reinforcement of the people around me. To make them stick.

*Lewis*: We've talked of this before. I think it's a good idea if anyone is interested to include a picture in their email or any site where you can add a photo. I think it would help you.

*Jean*: A voice is better. A phone call. Though I do get a flavor of the person's personality in texts and emails.

*Lewis*: I find it all very interesting. Back then, I wanted to learn more. With all that time in the car together, I had the opportunity to question you in more depth. Question after question. I think you found it good to discuss it with someone else, to work stuff out in your head.

*Jean*: For everyone I've told, you're the only one interested enough to dig deeper. And you're right; it has helped me learn more about myself, about Face Blindness, how to communicate it better to people, and how to make peace with it. Stuff like that.

*Lewis*: So that's how we became friends. It must have been strange for you, hopping into the car with a stranger at the beginning of the trip, and then, I'm sharing knowledge of stuff you had told me that you can't remember telling me. It must be weird.

*Jean*: The more you talk to me, the way you talk to me, the inflections in your voice will tell me if you are a friend or not. Because people who are friends will have a different inflection in their voice from people who are not friends. You have that inflection. Plus, I've heard your voice enough to know what level of friendship we hold. I would recognize your voice. That's how I know who you are. I may not remember everything we've done together, or what we've talked about, but once you start talking about the event, I will remember it. I might not have a picture in my head of you there. The reasoning part of me knows that you were there. So I will talk as if you were there.

*Lewis*: I wonder how easy it would be to imprint assumptions into your head…

*Jean*: You would like that, wouldn't you! I'll stop you from trying right now. Why? Because the brain is capable of amazing things. It will know something isn't right if you try to trick me, deceive me. Believe me, people have tried before. My brain will stick to the idea that something isn't right and won't let it go. It's a defense mechanism, maybe on a subconscious level. Where the Face Blindness won't let me retrieve the information I need, another part of my brain still knows that it's there and that something doesn't gel. You can call it a gut feeling or intuition. Whatever it is, it works. So, don't try it!

*Lewis*: Okay. Okay. I won't.

*Jean*: That's right: you won't.

*Lewis*: Come to think of it, I do remember a time when I had experienced your Face Blindness. I was walking with my wife outside *The Base,* the mall in Te Rapa in Hamilton. It must have been a holiday weekend. Heaps of people were shopping. Lee spotted you and Uwe walking towards us. We stopped and talked for a bit. You were quiet. Smiling. That, I do remember.

*Jean*: I was trying to place who you were. After you and Lee passed on, Uwe had to whisper, "That was Lewis, from your writers' group." It was before we had spent time together.

*Lewis*: I thought you looked vague. But I didn't think of it again until later when we talked in the car, and you brought it up. Another thing you had mentioned to me before is that you have to categorize people: who is important to remember, who is not. Because it's too hard to try to remember everyone. I must not have mattered much at that time.

*Jean*: Don't say that.

*Lewis*: Aw, just joking. You went on to say that if someone matters as far as importance goes, they will come back into your life.

*Jean*: It doesn't have to be a physical presence because the physical part of a person doesn't stay with me. I won't remember it. But the voice, I will remember and attach it to shared experiences.

*Lewis*: You say that I text the way I speak and that helps you. I call you *dude* and use all sorts of slang.

*Jean*: You're the only one who calls me dude, dude. And yes, your language is unique to you, which helps make it easier to distinguish you from others.

*Lewis*: You also are happy with me carrying on with all my

crazy stories.

*Jean*: That's because I like to put the burden of the conversation on the other person. Don't get me wrong, I do like your stories, too.

*Lewis*: Where I feel like I'm always firing questions back at you. It's all good fun. We're stuck in the car. No distractions. And we get to have some laughs, too. A good sense of humor is important in a friend. Don't always have to be serious.

*Jean*: Your stories do make me laugh... and cringe.

*Lewis*: Yeah. They make me cringe too. I don't understand why people find it hard to be your friend. I know you really struggle with that.

*Jean*: The difference with you is that you take the time to want to know me. You keep coming back. Most people find it too hard to *manage* me once I explain my limitations. That it takes more work than usual to be my friend. Part of the problem is that they don't truly comprehend. Friendship is two-sided. You give, and the other side gives. For me, it doesn't work that way. If you are not a constant in my life, I *will* forget you. I physically can't remember who you are. So you have to make the effort to stay connected to me. The other party has to give more.

*Lewis*: I don't see, on my part, where the extra work is coming in. It might just be my personality.

*Jean*: Most people who I would like to have as a friend, it's too hard for them.

*Lewis*: I don't understand that. I don't do anything particularly special to maintain our friendship.

*Jean*: Oh, but you do.

*Lewis*: I don't find it a chore to contact you. I don't think, *Oh, it's been a week, I'd better text Jean and touch base because she's going to forget me.* Sometimes months go by. It may be the next meeting or project, or when you house-sit that we will connect again. You never say, "Who are you?"

*Jean*: I call you a constant figure. I have to admit something. Doing this project, I had to come up with friends to be interviewed. It was really tough to get someone to agree, people that I thought were my friend. Not that you were my last choice. It's just that we've had the most intimate conversations out of everyone that I can *remember*. I think that's what real friendship means.

*Lewis*: I can see why you'd be sad about it. In all my interactions with you, I can't see how people would take your Face Blindness as an affront. Or the way you have to deal/cope with people in general. I think it comes down to that most people can't fully comprehend what is going on with you. Because when I did the interview with your boss, Katie, I've felt guilty ever since.

*Jean*: Why? She never said anything untoward.

*Lewis*: After we made the recording, I said to Katie that after a week or so, it's like everything goes away for you. I could see on her face that she found it quite a disturbing concept. Very disturbing. Afterward, I thought about how you don't like to be portrayed as weak or having these things that you cannot do because you like being a capable person. And in saying that to Katie, I felt I might have betrayed you somehow because I had made you look weak in your boss's eyes.

*Jean*: Katie did come up to me after the interview and tried to apologize for the things she had said.

*Lewis*: I wonder if she was saying, "I never realized this was the way things were for you," and I worried that she would look at you and think, *Can I trust her as much in what she is doing?*

*Jean*: There's nothing wrong with my intellect. Katie knows that.

*Lewis*: I know that, but I did feel guilty about revealing that to her.

*Jean*: I don't think Katie really fully understood the degree of my Face Blindness before her interview. She's read up on it medically, but experiencing it first hand is a whole different matter.

*Lewis*: Because it's so alien to people unless it's clearly explained. Even then, I think them not understanding is a safeguard to you. It's like in science fiction: an alien is like a human in a funny suit. But the one thing most sci-fi doesn't get is how their thinking would be alien and not human in the least.

*Jean*: My husband does say that I'm an alien.

*Lewis*: You're thinking would be alien to other people, the way you approach all relationships, because of what you need to do to cope. You're trying to mimic what others do naturally.

*Jean*: Very perceptive, Lewis

*Lewis*: I try to work out if there are ways I can trigger responses from you to help you figure out our level of friendship. Maybe retelling something personal from your life that you've shared with me. So that you can think, *Okay, I must've told this person this story, so there must be a certain level of friendship and trust with this person.* That's something I've been thinking of lately.

*Jean*: That's what makes you a proper friend. Because you are thinking of me and how to deal with me. Whereas most people, that doesn't enter their mind, even after I've told them my problem. I look normal. I behave normal. So, to them, the problem doesn't exist. No matter how many times I explain that it's there, in their mind, it doesn't exist. That's what makes the difference between a real friend and not.

*Lewis*: It always comes back to the voice. I find that interesting. You're not physically blind, yet your sense of hearing picks up where the brain can't 'see.' Since doing this book, you've said that you've become more aware of how important voice recognition is to you.

*Jean*: It has been good in many ways. I've been able to self-analyze my condition and how I function on a day-to-day basis.

*Lewis*: On my part, it's been interesting to see it unfold, to be a part of the process. We've had the ideal conditions for building a friendship. 1) Over an extended period of one to three-hour road trips of one-on-one conversations, 2) Fairly meaningful interactions, and 3) Consistency. We have a common interest in writing. We talk about it heaps.

*Jean*: It's not like I'm analyzing every person. In a few seconds, my brain will have established if someone is a friend or not. It may take longer to figure out how close a friend. I've become more analytical because I want to understand the disorder on a deeper level so that I can portray it better and more meaningfully to others.

*Lewis*: Even now, I still don't completely understand the disorder. I first understood it was you forget what you've done with a person. So when you see them, you don't recognize them because you don't remember that you've ever done anything with them. Now, I know it's not quite like that. You remember events. You remember everything around you, all the details. But for some reason, you don't see the people. They cease to exist. You'll remember that you came to my house and that I was here, but you won't have a face in your head. A body on the couch, just a presence, but no details. Weird, huh.

*Jean*: I'll give you an example. Both of us were at the Sir Julius Vogel awards ceremony last year. I remember the layout of the room, the stage, the round tables with tablecloths, bar table, doors, windows, what I was wearing – all those types of details. I remember where I was sitting and that each table held eight people. But ask me who was sitting with me at my table? I don't have a clue. In my head, the ballroom is empty of people. Oh, I can place shapeless forms around me, but not people. Logically, I know you were there. Were you sitting at my table? No? See, I can't remember. If I look at you now, I see your face. I close my eyes; you are wiped away. My head is a blank canvas. I can't remember what you look like. Open my eyes again, and there you are. It's even worse if people change the way they look. I may have drummed it into my head that this certain person has long brown hair, and then, they cut it. Yes, it's still brown, but now she's a whole new person to me. The best way I can describe it is that instead of people having a physical form, they have a persona, an entity that is defined by their voice.

*Lewis*: Wow! I learn something new about Face Blindness each time we get together and talk about it. Cool!

*Jean*: Let's say, for example, I attend a star-studded event. Famous actors, directors, and writers are there. I may recognize a voice and maybe a movie or television show an actor has played in or wrote, but that's all. Everyone in the room would be treated the same, from the lowly attendant to some hotshot movie star. As if I were talking to a person on the street or in the grocery line. Everyone sits on the same plane of existence in my head. It's a great leveler.

*Lewis*: Another superpower!

*Jean*: Ha ha. You're right; there are good points to having Face Blindness. When I'm in public, and there is a certain level of expected behavior to maintain, I find it takes a lot of work and a certain amount of stress and pressure to fit in. But when I'm with you, I don't have to pretend or wear that persona of normality. I am who I am. My problems. My faults. My superpowers. And it's okay. That's what friendship means.

*Lewis*: We are good friends as friends can be when it's a male/female friendship and not married to each other. We get work done. Or should I say - you get more work done. We have some laughs, share some experiences, yet know our place and go no further. Not that you would.

*Jean*: I would not cross that boundary. You know how insecure I am on the topic of friendship. That's why I'm going to ask, am I worth having as a friend?

*Lewis*: You don't need to ask that question. I don't waste my time on people not worth it. I only spend time with people I enjoy.

*Jean*: Aw, thanks.

*Lewis*: I still want to trick you out, though.

*Jean*: Go ahead and try, Lewis. Go ahead and try.

Thirteen:

# Analysis

*"Alone is what I have. Alone protects me."*

*Sherlock Holmes in* Sherlock: The Reichenbach Fall
*— screenplay by Stephen Thompson*

In preparation for this book, I was interviewed along with the other participants. It was a difficult but enlightening process. Difficult in that it brought back how much I had missed out in life, especially when it came to relationships. Enlightening in that it opened my eyes, not only to the perspectives of others of me and Face Blindness, but in the way I see myself. It forced me to grow as a person, and that's a good thing.

In our lives, we are surrounded by people. Friendship is one of the main fabrics of life. Though I have struggled since childhood to connect with people, I still feel the need for human interaction. My notes on the subject are extensive, too much to cover in the preceding chapters. Some gaps have been left. To bridge those gaps, more explanation was needed.

~

**You talked about coping mechanisms. How do you use them when it comes to building friendships?**

I wasn't aware that I was using coping mechanisms until

I was diagnosed with Face Blindness. Before this time, I very rarely said names. Later, I depended on my husband to fill in the gaps. When I learned of my disorder, I felt worse for a time. It's easier to think, *Oh, I can't remember people's names*, and be like everyone else, than to have a brain disorder where *I really can't* remember people *and* their names. In my adulthood, I went through bouts of loneliness, like I didn't have any friends, even though the logical part of me told me that I did. Then, I'll say, "Nah. I'm okay on my own. I'm happy in my self-contained world. I've managed this far without a friend." I have my husband.

**Don't you miss not knowing you have friends?**

How can I miss what I don't remember? However, there's an external influence where others talk about their friends, what they've done together, the fun they've had, or how they've shared experiences – good and bad. Sometimes, it makes me sad. I am the outsider. I know I have friends. Yet I cannot feel that end of it, the emotional attachment. For this book, I was asked to line up some friends to be interviewed. Do you know how hard that was for me to do? To figure out who was a friend? Who was not? And not just anyone, but someone who really knows me. What do I say to people? "Are you my friend? Do you know me well?" Yeah, that would go over great. You understand my dilemma.

I'm not saying I can't remember any friends. I do have a couple I remember for very specific reasons.

**What about keeping a friend diary?**

I think, in part, it was not wanting to admit I needed help. The other part was feeling a bit odd about keeping track of people. What would they think if they knew I was doing that – keeping a record of what we talked about, what we did together, their responses, some indication of the emotion of the experience. A log. Data. Lots of data.

When I think of how I would feel if someone did that to me, I wouldn't like it. Kind of creepy. That's what holds me back from doing it. It feels so impersonal. Like data gathering of a machine. Cambridge Analytica did that recently using Facebook and other platforms and got into big trouble. I don't know; I guess I could ask their permission first. But then I have the problem of recalling that we have a history, to begin with. Therein lies the conundrum.

**How does the lack of connection affect your conversation with people?**

I really miss intimate conversations. Let me clarify that: I miss the remembrance of intimate conversations. I must have them. I cannot be that banal. Yet I do protect myself when it comes to conversations with people. I struggle to recall what we might have talked about before. I risk the chance of looking stupid by repeating the same things to them. So, it's easier to keep conversations neutral, on subjects that are recent. Either that or I throw the burden of the conversation onto them.

I don't talk about my feelings with people. Say, I've shared a personal problem with someone. Later, the problem is fixed. But I can't remember that I've shared the problem with them in the first place, so I don't tell them it is fixed. They are still thinking the problem is there. It leaves me vulnerable. So, it's easier not to share. I feel uncomfortable keeping a log of such intimate details. If someone else read it, it would cause all sorts of problems. It's too hard. I put *having friends* in the *too hard basket*. It stressful being so limited – so deficient.

**What if you speak up about what you need?**

In general, I don't care what people think of me. I function on a day-to-day basis. Yesterday, last week, the people in those days are forgotten. It is today that matters.

Today, I met you. Today, I know you. As I've pointed out, friendships are hard for me to maintain. Very stressful when it should be relaxed and fun. You want me to ask people, *Are we good friends? Do you know me well? Do we have fun together? Do we speak about things that go on in my life? Your life?* It's so in their face! It's a weird way to maintain a friendship, don't you think? I want it to be natural. But I can't have that, can I?

Does that mean I should codify friendships? Make lists. Give instructions to people. Give them a chart showing where they will be in my mind in a day, a week, a month? Make them aware and give them an option to proceed or not? Seems so clinical.

When you observe me in a group, what do you see?

**In a social setting, your comments are neutral. You're moderately interactive when you have a specific role. You are very 'take charge' to the point that everyone is included, and the objective keeps moving in a non-confrontational manner. Running smoothly.**

I have no problem when it comes to having an objective, such as running the SpecFicNZ writers' group. I have clear goals to accomplish. This is different from having to manage a friendship. A big part of friendship is about saying to the person, *This is what I need from you.* Or feeling comfortable enough to ask, *This is bothering me. Can we talk about it?* It is a spirit of the core. Working together to build something together.

Part of the fear for me is repeating myself because I can't remember if I had already told this person the story or not. I need them to feel free to stop me. It takes honesty and trust to have that kind of relationship.

I classify myself as a high-maintenance friend. For the other person, it may feel a bit one-sided. If they don't understand that will be the case... well, I find that they don't stick around.

Now though, I'm very vocal about it. I will tell people upfront that I have Face Blindness and what it means. That if they see me again, I won't remember them until I learn their voice. That they need to keep telling me their name and feeding me information as to what we've done together or talked about. If they want to be my friend, they have to understand what they have to do to maintain it. Some do. Most don't. It's too much work for them.

I think I'm a likable person. I have much to offer in a friendship. I do care about them when I'm with them.

There is a part of me going, 'I want to have this friendship thing because I feel I need it.' However, there is another part that fights it. 'Why should I put any effort into this friendship when I won't remember it anyway?'

It's a real struggle. I feel like I make a lousy friend.

**That's not what I hear. Is it possible you may have an unrealistic view of friendship?**

Probably. I try to be a good person, a good listener. I don't have the ability to connect the same way with people as others do. But I'm not alone in that. Others have problems. They may have had difficulties in life that prevent them from connecting with others in certain ways – emotionally, physically, etc.

The key is the word *feel*. I *feel* like I make a lousy friend.

Can I get to know people well? No. But I can give to the friendship to the best of my ability with help. I know I have a lot to offer. I'm a giving person. I want to make people happy. That's the fixer in me. It's an integral part of my personality.

I *think* I can't be a good friend because I can't give the emotional component that comes with long-term friendships.

Or the reciprocation. I'd be thinking, *I should be doing something with this person*, and then, the thought is gone. The memory of the person is gone. I probably should write such things down, to remember that it was important. Again, it gets into that creepy zone. However, if I think about it, isn't that what the brain does? Make notes? Hmmm… interesting.

But I keep coming back to the lack of an emotional attachment.

## Emotional attachment?

Remember that I live in the day. Not yesterday's memories. Even with the use of notes, as far as my emotional response at the time, it will not help me *feel* anything for that person in the future. It leaves me neutral. It doesn't fix the underlying sense of loneliness. You need memories to fix that.

## You don't come over as a lonely person…

The natural tendency would be to isolate oneself. It is safer. Easier. However, I don't like easy. I want to be normal. So, I *make* myself be social. The more events – association with people and friends – that happen, the happier I am. Or if not happy, content. Not that I'll actually remember who was there. If it's with the same people/person over and over again, the more likely that memory will stay with me. But you have to keep in mind, if I lose contact with someone for a month or longer, they are gone from my memory. It has to be a regular thing. Even once a week, or a text with a photo of your face attached, or emails, Facebook, or Skype calls where I see you, etc. All those make a difference.

It takes a lot of effort to be in a group of people. My brain has to work overtime gathering information while others can go about the room talking with ease. I will paste on a happy face, of lightness and eagerness. But it's a ruse. Another coping mechanism. If you only knew the pressure I feel behind the smile on my face…

And through it all, I still keep trying.

**You mentioned the SpecFicNZ writers' group. Considering your problem with Face Blindness, how did that happen?**

I started writing professionally after we moved to New Zealand. I needed to make connections in the writing community. SpecFicNZ is a national writing association that caters to the speculative fiction writer – that is, science fiction, fantasy, and horror. I write science fiction and young adult fantasy. So, naturally, I joined up. However, I quickly learned that, unlike the U.S., where the population makes it easy to find a local writers' group, New Zealand doesn't have that – the population.

You know that saying (I think it came from the movie Robots) 'See a need; fill the need.' Well, I saw a need and volunteered to run a local SpecFicNZ writers' group in my area. My 'area' takes up the whole central part of the North Island. It's huge!

Talk about being out of my comfort zone. That first meeting was very difficult because I had no identifying markers as to who was who. I had only had email contact with Lewis. When I had set up that first meeting in a café, I gave Lewis identifying marks because that's how I function. I needed Lewis to find me because, when I walk in, I won't be able to distinguish him from the other patrons. Lewis told me later, once he got to know me, that he thought the situation unusual and the way I communicated how to spot me was odd. He understands now.

I've been organizing the meetings for about seven years now. Our group has grown from two to up to twenty.

**How do you manage to remember so many people?**

I don't. I keep a list of names and send out notices by email. I ask for RSVPs, not only so that I know how many will be attending, but also for me, so that I can prepare ahead of time to remember them. I've learned specific behavior patterns and qualities of the regulars. Once I figure out who is who in those first few minutes, I can put the voice and behavior pattern with that person.

When people don't hide who they really are and what they think, this is very helpful to me. Those strong personalities stick inside my head and will resurface more easily. Hopes, dreams, and contributions of all in attendance make us a well-rounded group of writers and, for me – friends. Progressing as a writer is one off-shoot of managing the group. The other is having a sense of belonging. Watching others grow as writers brings me great joy and satisfaction – that I've had a share in their lives.

At this point, they all know that I have Face Blindness and tease me continually.

**Do you mind? The teasing?**

No. It makes me feel that I am liked, even if the memory might not last. Don't friends tease each other?

**Yes, they do.**

Recently I did a presentation on Face Blindness and Writing Characters. I was talking about how I love writing science fiction and YA fantasy, and how I felt at home at such events like Comic-Con where everyone wears a costume. "My tribe," I said. One of the attendees made an interesting observation. He stated that maybe I was drawn to those genres – science fiction and fantasy – because they focused more on costumes, alien features and behavior, and those were things that I could remember over people's faces. It took me aback. He was right. Why didn't I notice that before? It makes so much sense.

**What about when someone comes to your home? That must be interesting.**

Yeah, that's a tricky one. As in all cases, I have to figure out who the person is. Sometimes it's easy, like the courier or a tradesperson. The uniform gives it away. If I'm expecting someone particular, I will assume the person at the door is him/her. It's when I have no clue who it is that it becomes interesting. In those first few moments, when the door opens, my brain is doing its thing. In a matter of seconds, I've registered body language, facial expression, and any external objects of note that might clue me in.

In those few seconds, when I have to decide whether I know them or not, I might recognize that I've had some interaction with this person before. It might be that they are weird, and it seems familiar. Or they're entertaining or open of face, and I can find a marker in that. Something not related to the face. I'm hopeless with faces.

Or maybe they are quite strange, and I wonder where this conversation is going. Every time that door opens, it's like starting over. I try to view it as an adventure instead of a problem. Makes for some interesting encounters.

**And when you are about town?**

Another tricky area. Normally, I don't pay attention to people. I'm not saying I'm not aware that they are there. They may be all around me, but unless I need to meet someone, my brain shuts off the need to identify people. It's a useless exercise. I'm constantly observing people, just not *seeing* them. Oh, I get caught out more times than I can count. I'd be in the grocery line, at the mall, or at a concert, or movie theater, and someone would be calling to me.

So, yes, I can say I've had some interesting experiences with people I know. That's why I've become more vocal about the disorder, so that people who know me can understand when I walk past them or don't acknowledge them. They know then that I'm not being snobbish. It stops a lot of negative talk about me.

I have a story for you.

I was at San Diego Comic-Con in 2013. Movie stars were everywhere. The chances of seeing someone famous were very high. When you can brag to your friends, *Guess who I saw!* Do you think I could pick the actors out? *No!* Not even the ones who were in normal clothes. That sucks! Though I did come home with one special photo.

Almost everyone wears a costume. It's a fantastic thing to see. I wore a sexy steampunk outfit.

Anyway, I saw several people dressed as *Loki* walking around. One was particularly well done. I asked the person if I could take a picture. He said, "Yes," and posed with his Tesseract staff in that famous Loki pose. I didn't find out it was Tom Hiddleston in full costume until a few weeks after I had flown back home. He was there for a panel promoting *The Avengers* and *Thor: The Dark World* and had said that he had been on the main floor mingling with the attendees. One of them was *me*, and I didn't know it! So disappointing. Though I do have the picture… Yes, I am bragging… a little. Well, maybe, a lot.

**What would you say is the biggest thing that has helped you deal with your disorder when it comes to friendships?**

That's easy. Social media.

Think about it. Before social media, we were dependent on the telephone for communication. Or physically meeting up. The chances of constant communication were slim. Now with social media – Facebook, Instagram, Snapchat, to name a few – we are bombarded with pictures and updates. This might annoy some. For me, it's a lifesaver. The more I see someone online, the more they talk about their life, the better chance I may recognize them when meeting. The same idea with the little picture attached to text messages, Google pages, and emails. All these avenues help connect me to people. All are markers.

Though I do depend on voice recognition, it doesn't hurt to have a repertoire of other means for memory recall. I need all the help I can get, and still, it may not be enough.

So, thank you, social media. Thank you for being in my face. The bane of some people's lives is my savior. When you want to smash all those annoying apps, think of me. And maybe send me a photo and a message. ☺

## Fourteen:

# The Brother – Jeff

*"I want to do something splendid... something heroic or wonderful that won't be forgotten after I'm dead. I don't know what, but I'm on the watch for it and mean to astonish you all someday."*

*Jo March in* Little Women *by Louisa May Alcott*

*Jeff*: You and I have talked several times through the years about Face Blindness. I thought I had Face Blindness, too. We've shared some things that we haven't shared with anyone else. Because who do we know who would understand it? It felt good to talk about it with someone. And I trust you.

*Jean*: Thank you, Jeff. I feel the same way. A few years back, you told me that you were picked by a research team to study your condition.

*Jeff*: The study is through The Rotman Institute at the Baycrest Centre. The hospital is in the North York district of Toronto, Ontario, Canada. Baycrest is affiliated with the University of Toronto. Six of us went through extensive testing. Though I went in thinking I had Face Blindness, the doctors discovered that I had SDAM – Severely Deficient Autobiographical Memory. It's a mouthful, I know. On one of my visits, I had mentioned to the neuroscientist that you have Face Blindness. He found that interesting. I'm not sure if there is a relation between the two disorders. He didn't say, and I didn't ask.

*Jean*: I'll have to do some research and check the association. Can you define SDAM?

*Jeff*: The doctors are shy about calling SDAM developmental amnesia. But it's a form of amnesia – not being able to store memories. I can remember facts and figures, but not episodic memories.

*Jean*: Can you remember people?

*Jeff*: I have a tough time remembering people. I think you are worse than me. It gets awkward when they obviously remember me, and I don't remember them. However, I can recognize people if I've had frequent visits with them. I will somehow surmise that I know them. Names will come and go.

*Jean*: Will you recognize a voice?

*Jeff*: Only when I become very accustomed to someone.

*Jean*: I am dependent on audio. I tell people that I can only remember them if they keep talking to me over several occasions. It doesn't happen with one or two conversations. As for my brain, I have no people in my brain.

*Jeff*: I have nothing in my brain. It's proven. That's where SDAM differs from Face Blindness. I can't picture anything. I have no visual, audio, or oratory memory. I don't remember music or hear music in my head. And forget about remembering lyrics! It's impossible.

*Jean*: I have the same problem. I took voice lessons for years. Mostly Italian and musical theater. Do you think I could learn the lyrics of the songs? I'd have to sing them over and over and over again. And still… nope. Nothing.

*Jeff*: When people ask me what my favorite song is, I try to cover by just coming up with a random song, a go-to song.

I can't label it as my favorite song. It's a song to appease somebody with.

*Jean*: That's very interesting. There are similarities between the two disorders. With Face Blindness, the information is there; the retrieval process is missing. A disconnection.

*Jeff*: I believe it's the same with me. The interesting part with me is having no visual or audio memory. No pictures in my brain. Though I do have dreams.

*Jean*: You can remember your dreams?

*Jeff*: I remember certain facts for a brief time. I can't replay it, though. I will know, for example, it was like 'a horse chasing a buffalo.' Just being able to do that tells me that there is some connection that opens up during the sleep cycle. Do you have dreams?

*Jean*: I know I dream. I very rarely remember them. And if there were people involved, they won't have faces. I'll know who they're supposed to be, but they won't have a specific form.

*Jeff*: I have a general concept of people. I will know it's that person.

*Jean*: If I close my eyes, I don't see people.

*Jeff*: I have that, too.

*Jean*: When I look at someone, I can see their face. I know it's a face. Yet, I'm not really 'seeing' it. I look away, the person is gone from my mind.

*Jeff*: That sounds about right to me. Mine goes a bit farther with having no images in my head. The doctors think it may be linked to a condition called *Aphantasia*, where one does not possess a functioning 'mind's eye' and cannot voluntarily visualize imagery.

*Jean*: I definitely do not suffer from *Aphantasia*. It would cripple me.

*Jeff*: Enter my world.

*Jean*: Wow. When did you start feeling that something wasn't right?

*Jeff*: It was in my teenage years. Like you, I was quite intelligent.

*Jean*: You still are.

*Jeff*: I don't know about that. Back in high school, I was part of the top ten gifted and talented group. I was invited to attend Colgate University seminars with the other top students. One of the professors asked about visualization. Everyone raised their hands. So I did too, even though I couldn't visualize anything, because I wanted to fit in. Back then, I was thinking, *Why can't I do this when everyone else seems to be able to?* I became very curious about it. I don't think, at the time, it was much of an issue psychologically. It wasn't until a little bit later that it became a huge problem for me.

*Jean*: I remember that you became very depressed in your senior year.

*Jeff*: It was at the end of high school. High school was a stepping-stone to adulthood. I couldn't plan ahead. It was too much for my mind to deal with. I had no vision of the future. I still have no vision of the future. Everything I do, I do in the day. I throw myself into it both physically and emotionally and hope for the best. A lot of kids were going to college. I didn't have a plan. Mom and Dad were pressuring me to get a job. We lived in a depressed area. Combine all that with a bit of an issue with SAD (Seasonal Affective Disorder). That was because the winter season was so long – sometimes lasting six months or more. You probably remember how short the days were and how it seemed to go on forever. Being stuck inside the house. It made me very depressed. I knew it was because of my stupid brain. I had no one to talk to who could possibly understand that. Even the doctors I saw looked at me dumbfounded as if it couldn't be true.

*Jean*: I handled it by acquiring an eating disorder. I didn't know what was wrong with me. I had no clue about Face Blindness. Did you have problems with relationships like I did?

*Jeff*: It makes it very difficult to have relationships with other people, especially building lasting bonds. Any bonds I have made are only due to the fact that, somehow, we were thrown together for a period of time where we could get to know each other. If I were meeting for the first time, say, a woman, I might think, *Wow! She's beautiful. I like her.* But then, I walk away, and I have no attachment anymore. She's gone from my memory, and you can't build on that. It's only when you are constantly together that you come into a relationship with others.

*Jean*: That's very similar to Face Blindness. I really struggle with friendships because I can't remember the person. I can't remember if I've had a particular conversation with that person already. It's a dilemma.

*Jeff*: Me too. Now, I'm almost silent because I'm afraid to talk to people. I worry that I've already had that conversation with them. Telling the same story over and over again. Like an old person.

*Jean*: Me, too. Wow! How do you feel about family?

*Jeff*: I don't know what to tell you there. I get a sense that I love my family, but at the same time, there is a distance because I can't grasp our relationship. For example, I know you are my sister but, because I hardly see you, you're out of my mind. I don't have the attachment like others have.

*Jean*: I explain it like this: I don't have any attachment because I don't have the memory, which is the foundation for building attachments. That's why I question love. I don't know if I love because love is built upon the same premise. You don't love someone at the first meeting. It just doesn't happen. And for me, it is a first meeting most of the time. So, how do I know if I love someone? I really struggle with that.

*Jeff*: I can feel something for someone. Love. I just don't have the memory as to why I feel that way.

*Jean*: I have no attachment to anyone.

*Jeff*: That's sad.

*Jean*: I know. But the good thing is I can't hate either.

*Jeff*: That's one way to look at it. I'm the same. They can do something awful to me, and I won't remember it. I can hate someone in the present, but I can't hold onto that feeling.

*Jean*: Emotions and feelings are two separate entities. An emotion is in the present. Someone does something to you and it hurts. That is in the moment. A feeling would be a grudge or resentment based on memories of the event. Love is also a feeling. Real love is based on building blocks of memories. The only way I got married was because of a long-distance relationship made up of letters and phone calls. A face wouldn't have helped me.

*Jeff*: I could never do that. Because I need a real person, or I'd be stuck with my inner thoughts. My head is empty of visuals. I have a severe sense of loneliness like I need someone, but at the same time, I keep picking the wrong people. I think it's a part of me that's not looking for a realistic relationship. I think I am afraid of a relationship even though I want one so severely. It's because I don't know how I'm going to react on a day to day basis with someone else.

*Jean*: With Uwe, I know that he is going to come home every day because we are married. As far as feelings go, I try not to think about it, or it gets depressing.

*Jeff*: I don't make any future plans as far as marriage is concerned. I can't even conceive myself as being there. I

believe in concepts such as loyalty and keeping a vow –
those types of institutional structures.

*Jean*: I do, too. What about coping mechanisms?

*Jeff*: I mostly fabricate things. Like with the song or when they
want to talk about memories of something. I'll tell some
story that might not even be true. It's difficult.

*Jean*: I'm with you. Have you considered using a note system
to help your memory? Writing down the name and why.
Or the date and why. That's how I keep track of some
stuff.

*Jeff*: I rely on just remembering, and then… don't. (laughs)
I'm fearful of growing older, of what I'm going to be like.
It's not going to be pretty.

*Jean*: I don't think it's pretty for anyone.

*Jeff*: You should contact the people I went to see. It might be
interesting to talk to them about your case.

*Jean*: I will do that. There is a common connection between
the two. Maybe something familial, too. I'll keep you
posted.

Fifteen:

# Work

*"Oh, you hate your job! Why didn't you say so? There's a support group for that. It's called everybody, and they meet at the bar."*

*Drew Carey, comedian*

When it comes to the workforce, I've worn a variety of hats over the years. Face Blindness can be managed or camouflaged in most circumstances. The brain finds a way to cope or mask the problem that comes with a lack of facial recognition. Most of the time, the sufferer doesn't even know this process is going on. It wasn't until I became aware of the disorder that I took note. By this time, I had already held a few positions.

When I was young, I worked as a chambermaid at a motel in Bolton Landing, New York, a popular tourist destination for those who lived in New York City. It was hard work. In the morning, the manager would hand out a list of rooms to each employee. Ten rooms was the standard number for a day's work. Once the rooms were assigned, I had minimal contact with people for the rest of the day. Knowing names wasn't essential or even necessary.

It's amazing how easy it is to get away without saying a person's name in a conversation. Sometimes it only takes a touch of their sleeve to get their attention. Or to catch their eye to converse. I made no connections with the other women even though we ate lunch together every day. Back then, I blamed it on my shy nature, plus they were much older than me, and I felt we had nothing in common but the job. I worked for the hotel for one season and then, we moved to New York's capital city, Albany.

In my next job, after a brief stint at childcare, I worked as a receptionist/secretary for an automotive pin-striping company. The position consisted of taking jobs over the phone, organizing the tasks for the boss and his two helpers each day, and booking the work. People were names on pieces of paper and voices over the phone. The guys came in only to restock their trucks. Again, I had minimal contact with anyone. It was perfect; not that I had realized it at the time.

Then came the years of raising children. It was during this time that I learned that I had Face Blindness and my perception of my relationship with people changed. Entering the workforce again presented new challenges. Awareness isn't always a good thing. With that awareness came a sense of insecurity. Can I manage to work with people? Will they notice that something is wrong with my memory? Can I hide it? Do I hide it? All these questions raced through my mind.

However, there came a point when we needed more income. Kids are expensive. The two older children were in elementary school and the youngest was a three-year-old.

Nine years had passed since I left the workforce. My past work experience was limited. I felt inadequate to even apply for positions. Nonetheless, a job was a necessity, and so I put myself out there. Fortunately, a position came up where my youngest brother, Jeff, worked. It was because of him that I got the job. I didn't even have to interview for the position. Someone was listening to my prayers.

The company was a sales and repair/warranty service

shop for outdoor power equipment. My position revolved around data entry and creating a paper trail for parts ordered over the phone. I'd type up the orders, then enter them into the system. They'd print out in the warehouse for picking and shipping. If I made a mistake putting in the wrong number code, which I did once in a while, I'd have to run to the warehouse and catch the slip before the guys packed it. The only people I came in contact with were the few workers in the front office. Again, their names weren't important to me. I used the same diversion tactics that my brain had established long before I knew about the Face Blindness. Nobody in the office knew I had a problem, and I liked it that way.

All was good for a few years. I had no high expectations. I was happy to be gaining some experience in the workforce, even if it wasn't a challenging job.

One thing I've learned is that life never stays the same. Life is all about the change and how you embrace it – or not. Our circumstances were about to change again, and so was my career.

The printing companies in Utica were struggling. The whole area had been hit by a recession. There was talk of lay-offs. The other big printing company was already letting people go. Uwe and I knew that it was only a matter of time before his shop would be doing the same. We decided to be pro-active, but that meant moving again.

Uwe found a job in Troy, New York, which was near Albany. The recession had not hit that area as hard as it had hit the central part of the state. My younger brother, Roger, and his family lived in Cohoes, a neighboring suburb. I was happy to move close to them because I knew them and didn't need to work hard to establish new connections. It was through my brother's wife that I started on a new career path – dentistry. That was twenty-some years ago.

When I took the position as a dental assistant, I thought nothing of how much it entailed interacting with people. Not just the doctor and the staff but, more importantly, the patients. Some of the tactics I had used before didn't work in this new environment. It left me feeling vulnerable, but I was determined to persevere.

This particular dental office was a large practice: two dentists, four hygienists, three dental assistants, and four office staff. Needless to say, the waiting room was always busy. The assistants were called upon to bring the patients back to the treatment rooms. I didn't think it would be a problem for me. I was so wrong.

The dentists kept the patients' files for the day in the treatment rooms, which was a common practice. The problem came when I had to remember the next patient's name from the treatment room all the way to the waiting room, which was, in my mind, a long way away. Down the long hall, through two doors, past the main office and around the corner, I would be silently repeating the name over and over again. Most of the time I would get it right, and someone would stand and follow me. But that wasn't always the case. Even repeating the name didn't guarantee I would remember it by the time I made it to the waiting room. You have to keep in mind that my brain can't recall faces. Even for repeat patients.

There I was, looking helplessly at those sitting in the waiting room. I felt like a fish out of water. My lips were moving, but nothing was coming out. And my eyes were wide with fright. Then came the embarrassing swivel, back to the office to ask for the patient's name.

While I was conscious of my blunders and embarrassed by them, I never knew if anyone else cared or not, or even noticed.

That first dental practice taught me a lot, not just about the medical profession but about how to manage my disorder and how to deal with people on a daily basis. It would've been so easy to walk away from such a people-orientated occupation. For someone with Face Blindness, it's not an obvious career choice. It's like a deaf person choosing to work in an audio store. Small or large, the size of the practice doesn't matter. The problem remains the same.

You would think I would've given up on it as a career, given the daily complications. But I'm not that kind of person, especially now that I've moved into oral surgery. The opportunity came up, and I took it. Every new path is an adventure. You never know where those paths will lead. And if you don't take them, how much of life will you miss.

I thought that first practice I worked at was large. My current position in an oral maxillary surgeons' practice makes that office look small. It also makes my Face Blindness a bigger problem. With four surgeons and one pediatric dental specialist, five to six office staff, six to eight nurses, and two dental assistants, it is daunting to try to remember everyone, especially when the nurses are not on the same schedule as me. People are coming and going. Some of the staff have babies and leave, then come back. Add in all the patients for that number of doctors, and you can see my problem: people overload.

Yes, I use the same tactics: reading name badges, listening for others to say names, or finding a way not to have to use a name. In the case of patients, I try to read it from their file, or off the day sheet, the computer, or monitors – anywhere my eye can glance without the patient knowing what I'm doing.

None of this affects my work performance. My job isn't about saying a name. It's about specific skillsets and functioning competently, efficiently, and safely in the medical environment, whether in theater at the hospital or in the clinic at the office. Surgical and clinical procedures are both defined by medical knowledge and a trained skillset. Face Blindness has nothing to do with intelligence. My case proves that. I can't remember a face, but I have no problem remembering the procedures needed for my job. I'm not bragging, just stating a fact.

However, the issues surrounding Face Blindness have come up in the workplace. I can give a couple of examples.

I work with four surgeons and with Katie, the pediatric dental specialist. I've been working with Katie for fourteen years and spend most of my work time with her. That means working with children, which in turn creates a specific problem. Because children are growing, they are continually changing. You may not notice or think of it at all: you may easily recognize them as they become taller, thinner or fatter, and their faces and voices change and mature. It's a nightmare for me. Add in glasses or braces, or changing bodies such as breasts and curves, or sprouting facial hair, and I am totally lost. And I've *chosen* to work in this field. I know: I'm crazy.

When the children come back for their appointments at six-month intervals, it's like they're a whole new person. What saves me is that Katie has always made it a practice to go down to the waiting room to get the patient. It's her way of making the children feel at ease – meeting her first. Since they are children, a parent or two, some siblings, or grandparents usually come along. It makes for a full clinic. In this situation, I don't even try to remember names.

Katie usually takes responsibility for the conversation. She will remember the social and family aspects of the children and their parents. I won't recall any of that, even if they've been coming for years. My contribution to the conversations will center on the present, such as the weather, or something mundane – their new shoes, shirt, cute braids, haircut, their growth (even if I haven't noticed it myself), the special stuffed animal they brought along… I have a whole list of talking points that I can select from. In all this, I still won't recognize the child or the parents.

Another problem arises if I have to get the patient. On one occasion, Katie asked me to get the patient because she was behind in dictating notes and needed the extra few minutes to finish up. I took the chart. I opened to the name and checked the date of birth as a guide as to how tall I thought the child would be. In the waiting room, I will scan the people and find a child. If there's one child, everything is great. If there are several, and they look to be in the same age group, it could potentially spell trouble. I called out the patient's first name. A parent and the child got up and followed me back to Katie's room. All the while I was chatting away happily about nothing in particular. It wasn't until Katie came into the room and saw the child sitting in our blue treatment chair that I knew I had made a mistake. There had been two children in the waiting room with the same name and around the same age. Fortunately, the parent and Katie laughed it off. Though I hid it, I was mortified! Thank goodness I'm rarely called upon to get a patient.

I had told Katie about the Face Blindness disorder before this incident. I'm not sure she really understood it, even though she looked it up in medical journals. This was her first taste of how it affected my life: a small taste. It wasn't until a few years later when her eyes were truly opened.

Both Katie and I are fitness conscious. I knew Katie had a membership at the same local gym. One day, as was my routine, I got on a stationary bike to start with some cardio before moving later onto the free weights. There was a woman on the bike next to me, but I paid no attention and started my workout.

"Aren't you going to say hello?" she said.

I looked over, confused, trying to place the voice.

"Katie?" I asked, still unsure.

"Yes! You really don't recognize me?"

"Sorry. Your hair is tied up. You're in gym clothes. I wasn't expecting you." Which were all valid excuses.

"Wow," she said, "you really meant it when you said you couldn't recognize people."

I smiled, and said, "Not even you."

By this point, we had been working closely together for ten years. I think Katie thought that would make a difference.

Later, when we were back in the office, we talked about the incident. Katie had many questions. This time, she listened with care and really tried to grasp what it was like to live with the disorder. We still talk about it when Katie catches me out. Not that she does that often. It has become a quiet joke between us.

This isn't the first time I've been caught out in public. Besides friends and workmates, most of our patients reside in or around Hamilton. They may use the same grocery stores, post office, or shopping malls as I do.

"Hi, Jean."

I'll turn to find someone looking expectantly at me.

"Oh, hi," is my go-to response. Meanwhile, I'm thinking, *Oh boy. How do I know this person? They know me. They said my name.*

Are they a friend? A workmate? From the office? Someone from the private hospital? From church? A patient? A writer?

So stressful!

On my face resides a smile, but behind the eyes, my brain is working hard. All the while, I'm trying to ascertain from their body language and voice, where this person fits into my life. I hope that they will say something to trigger recognition, an anchor of a remembered event, but most of the time it doesn't happen. This leaves me floundering. Instead of getting caught out, I will try to end the conversation and move on. Not because I don't care, but because I am embarrassed for not knowing who they are.

The same questions happen when someone catches my eye or stops me and has a friendly smile on their face. The smile tells me that they must know me. But how well? I have to figure it out and fast.

If I am stuck and can't get away, I will come out and bluntly say, "Do I know you?"

It has happened a few times. I will be very apologetic.

"I'm sorry. I have this thing. It's called Face Blindness. I don't recognize people."

They will usually reply with the same old response, "I'm terrible with faces, too."

(Sigh)

At the end of the conversation I will conclude with a smile and say, "It was nice talking to you anyway."

What more can I do?

If they're a patient, I don't feel as bad. It's not like I have a personal relationship with them. However, it's important to be friendly to everyone.

For the surgical side of my job, calling patients by their names is not relevant. Patients are wheeled into the operating theater on beds. Their wrist tags are compared to their medical file by the nursing staff. My job is setting up the instruments and equipment for the operation, assisting the surgeon during the surgery, and cleaning up afterward.

The problem comes when I need to get the attention of the circulating nurse or one of the other assisting staff members. I will be panicking, thinking, *What's her name? What's her name? What's her name?* while trying to remain outwardly cool and collected. Usually, I can get away without saying the name, but not always. There are many ways of getting a person's attention, and the coping mechanisms I learned earlier in life are lifesavers for me. I don't want the Face

Blindness to affect my work efficiency.

This particular problem has fortuitously been resolved without me having to say a word. A couple years ago, whiteboards were put up in all the operating theaters with a list of all the functioning positions. Before the beginning of surgery, the names of the anesthetist, anesthetist technician, doctor, nursing staff, and assistants are written beside the appropriate positions. All I have to do is glance at the board, and I have the name I need. Though we use the same anesthetists, the nursing staff is always changing. I'm incredibly grateful to whomever it was who organized the whiteboards. Thank you very much!

I've now been in the medical field for twenty-five years. Face Blindness has never been an issue where it has affected my job, the patient, or surgery. It doesn't make me less qualified. In the past, I didn't even think to bring it up because I never thought of it as an issue. I don't think it would have gone down well to say to the dentist or doctor, "Oh, by the way, I have Face Blindness. I won't remember your patients."

Besides, in the medical field, systems are set up to cover human error. As a responsible caregiver, I make sure that I'm not put in a position to cause any kind of medical error.

In the clinic, the doctor is in charge of the patient. I'm the secondary caretaker and the doctor's personal assistant. Surgeries done in the clinic, I play a third role. The nurses check patients in, clarifying their identity, and consent to the operation. While I do help to make the patient comfortable before the procedure, which includes small talk, my primary role is to set up for surgery, assist during the operation, then clean up afterward. I also become the dentist's second pair of eyes during surgery and am there to point out anything unusual and to maintain the patient's safety. The procedure is the same for general anesthetics. Assisting is one of the 'hats' I wear. And I wear it like a comfortable pair of old jeans.

~

The other hat I wear is as a writer. I love this job – writing. Why? For many reasons, but one of the most appealing ones for me is that I can work alone. No people. Just a laptop, my notes, and my vivid imagination.

In his book *On Writing: A Memoir of the Craft*, Stephen King said, "Writing is a lonely job." Though most writers would agree with that statement, I do not. I thrive on the isolation. I don't need people to be happy or for validation. I don't really care if they like what I write. I write because I love the process of creating something, of expressing myself through the characters on the page.

In fact, Face Blindness becomes a blessing. Well, isn't that a nice change!

Being alone with my thoughts, with the words flowing from my fingertips gives me great pleasure and a sense of well-being, much more so than being with people. People are hard work. I can never truly relax, whether at the clinic or hospital, socializing outside work, or with friends. Writing gives me freedom from those anxieties associated with Face Blindness.

As soon as I sit down, a calmness settles over me. I am my own master. I don't need anyone (or rarely). I can write for days, weeks, and be totally happy. A first draft may take me four months of my life. But I don't mind the isolation.

After making the statement about the loneliness of writing, Stephen King went onto say, "Having someone who believes in you makes a lot of difference. They don't have to make speeches. Just believing is usually enough."

I understand the logic behind the statement. Writing is like acting or any other type of art form: it is very intimate. You are exposing your inner self through your work. The world is full of critics and hard skeptics. Just go onto Twitter, Facebook, or other social media sites and look up your favorite actor, musician, or author, and you'll find them picked apart no matter how good their work or how successful they are. Having someone who believes in your talent goes a long way in keeping those hungry, egotistical critics in their place. I believe Stephen King; you don't need the whole world to like your work. One other person is enough to validate what you do.

I would be totally happy just to write. Though I love surgery, the constant stress of dealing with staff and patients can be draining. I'd give it up in a snap in order to spend more time in the career that I love. I am continually learning my craft, improving my skills as a writer, and gaining confidence. Perfection belongs to the angels. That doesn't mean I won't strive for it.

Yes, Face Blindness still gets in the way. However, I've learned how to make adjustments to compensate for my deficiency in remembering my own characters, the same as an actor would compensate for a stutter or learn a different way to remember their lines.

I use an extensive character bible that I create as part of the prep work for a novel or script. This is a separate book in which I create a breakdown of each character in the story.

There are four separate parts, the most extensive being the character description sheet. I usually pick out a photo of a person from the internet or from a magazine, concentrating on the face. This photo is pasted at the top of the sheet and represents how I would picture the character, if I could. Below that is an itemized list of features from head to toe. It includes things such as their handshake, laugh, posture, and mannerisms. I refer to these pages regularly as I write to help me put in the details that I can't remember and to keep the character consistent.

The next part deals with the internal workings of the character – their intellectual and emotional makeup – what makes them tick.

Another sheet asks questions about specific incidents in the character's life that have affected them and have shaped the person they are at the time of my story.

The last section is the backstory of the character. I start with any important details from the parents and grandparents that have an effect on the character and the story.

For each character, I may have four to eight pages of information. All the information is printed and put into a physical binder or saved in a character file kept on my laptop. For a trilogy, it's not unusual to have a hundred pages in that character bible. For me, it is compulsory, just as a script is compulsory for making a movie.

Writing is isolating, and that, for me, is one of its attractions. So, it's somewhat ironic that, yet again, I've chosen to pursue a more people-orientated approach to writing. For the past six years, I've been involved in helping young writers across New Zealand, through writing workshops and organizing annual short-story competitions for intermediate and secondary students. These competitions force me to deal with, not only the students but the parents and teachers, too. They have allowed me to give back to the community by taking my knowledge as a writer directly into schools. Such a contrary thing for someone with Face Blindness to do – workshops with strangers. I must be a glutton for punishment.

Needless to say, the future is a blank page. I'm excited to see what life will imprint in my personal book. Hopefully, it will be well-written.

Sixteen:

# The Boss – Katie

*"Everyone talks about building a relationship with your customer.
I think you build one with your employees first."*

*Angela Ahrendts (Senior Vice President, Apple)*

Jean and I have been working closely together for almost fourteen years. When I say closely, she is my dental assistant, so we are side-by-side for a large portion of the day. I am a Pediatric Dental Specialist. I have a private practice, but we also take on contracts in conjunction with the Waikato Hospital from time to time, when their lists are backlogged. Jean plays a key role in organizing my practice and also the general anesthetic cases undertaken at a private hospital.

In the beginning, we didn't socialize much outside the workplace. Jean was new to the country. She was quiet. I learned quickly that Jean had a strong work ethic. Still does. She is very loyal, trustworthy, kind, with a bubbly spirit, yet relatively quiet. She says what needs to be said.

I don't remember when Jean told me that she had Face Blindness. I don't think it was right away. Maybe a couple of years after we'd been together. I wouldn't have picked it up if she hadn't said anything. Even then, I can't say that it has ever impacted her ability to do her job or affected her job performance. We've been working together for so long; we are used to each other's ways, like an old married couple. Jean's very good at knowing what I want even before I know it. That's a real skill, especially when it comes to four-hand dentistry and surgery. Not everyone can do that; think that far in advance.

It would be hard for the average person to work out that Jean has Face Blindness. I think that she's adapted to it so well. Also, her being American might have thrown me off – mannerisms, terminology, and such. We don't know how someone's behavior is affected by their nationality, upbringing, and religion. So many factors are involved. You don't automatically realize that it may be due to a disability. Not that I think Jean is odd.

Our patient load is large. Some have been coming for years and years. I know that there are some that I wouldn't recognize too. My understanding is that Jean doesn't

"Nurse, I believe I've found the problem..."

recognize any of them.

From the beginning, I had made it a practice to greet the patient and bring them to our room. That's the way I like it. Even I sometimes struggle to know which child is which, especially if there are three or more, or twins. From my understanding, Jean has that struggle with everyone. The operational details of the practice, she can remember. But if I said, 'the blond-haired, blue-eyed child,' she wouldn't know who I was talking about.

There was one particular time that I can recall where I experienced Jean's Face Blindness first hand. It was at the gym. She didn't know me until I spoke. She can often recognize people by their voice. Obviously, when I come to work and walk in, she knows it's me. But if she sees me out of context, it might be harder. Like at the gym. Jean won't say hello. She treated me like a stranger. Once I said hello, she knew it was me. When this happened to me, there were two options: either Jean wanted to ignore me, or Jean didn't know who I was.

Jean is a very kind person. So, I knew that it couldn't be the first. She really didn't recognize me. Wow. That's the moment it truly hit me.

Jean's Face Blindness hasn't affected our relationship at all. We get along really well. I like her and value her opinions on things. We do chat a lot in the tearoom about family and what's happening in our lives.

As far as her job goes, I consider the blindness in her left eye more noticeable than her Face Blindness. If something drops on the floor, it takes Jean a moment to find it. I should mention, though, that the floor color doesn't help. Speckled gray. So, maybe it's not all her fault she can't see it. I'm teasing. Or, if she asks what tooth I'm working on, I attribute it to her sight. However, it could be the dentistry itself since it's tricky working in small mouths and looking around tight corners.

I didn't know anything about Face Blindness until Jean mentioned it. There was something on television about it, maybe two or three years ago, and I thought, *Oh, that's what Jean's got!* I don't know if I would have paid attention otherwise.

I know that her brother has it too and is involved in some medical studies. His is more severe than Jean.

We were talking about her Face Blindness the other day, and about her writing – how she can't visualize her characters and has to keep a book with each of her characters mapped out. As she writes, she has to go back and check what color hair, eyes, face, etc. Writing is hard enough without having to worry about that. She told me that when she dreams, she doesn't see faces, just bodies. I've never come across anyone else before with Face Blindness. I've never read about it. I think this book is a great idea.

Were there any tell-tale signs in the beginning? When we first met, Jean had just arrived from America. I had come up from Dunedin to start a practice in Hamilton. My practice was fairly new when Jean started as my assistant. There was an adjustment period for both Jean and I, not only in getting to know each other but in building the practice. We had to get used to new families. Many of these children have been with us now for ten to thirteen years.

If I think back, it must have been difficult for Jean, not just dealing with new people, but a new culture and country. And our Kiwi accent. Or I should say, we had to get used to her 'funny' accent. (I'm teasing again.)

When you meet someone new and have to work closely with them, it can be a challenge. The first thing I had to work out was her religious background. Before we moved into our permanent rooms, we worked out of another practice. When it was someone's birthday and cake was served, Jean would discreetly put her piece of cake back. I wondered why. From that, we had some interesting discussions about her religious background, and I understood. To be honest, her religious beliefs affect her working life just as much as Face Blindness or her vision.

I love finding out about Jean's life. She's done an amazing array of things. When you talk to her about dogs, she's bred dogs. When you talk to her about chickens, she's had massive numbers of chickens. Scuba diving. Opera singing. Belly dancing. Motorcycles. (She used to come to work on her motorcycle.) Jean's been in commercials on television. Even on *Shortland Street*, New Zealand's local television soap. I have to laugh at that. Jean is a fascinating person. She's had her tough times, too.

All through this, you wouldn't have a clue Jean has Face Blindness. She doesn't let it affect her job or what she does in life. It doesn't slow her down one bit.

If I walk out of the room and come back... does Jean recognize me? Remember me? That's a difficult question. I don't know. I do know that Jean's not great with names. Even if she knows a person, she doesn't always remember their name. I'm not great at it, either. Cris – whom Jean job-shares with – she can tell you everybody's name and their family history. That can be really helpful having that kind of background. I guess some people are more interested in that as well. Jean's so dignified. She never wants to gossip. She may know some of the stuff but never lets on. Cris knows because she has grown up in this town.

Getting back to Jean's ability to do her job, she's incredible. You wouldn't get a better dental assistant. She knows exactly what I'm going to say to the patients and when. She can repeat my whole spiel without blinking an eye. She knows what I'm thinking of, what I'm going to do next, and what I'm going to need. I almost never have to ask her for anything. Jean just knows! From that perspective, we are obviously well-connected. To be a good dental assistant takes a lot of intuition.

Of course, Jean has been in the industry for years and years. Yet, you can have others who are not quite as responsive as that. And the patients and parents pick up on that. They're astounded by Jean's abilities. Every now and then, I try to catch Jean out. It's a bit of a joke between us. There will be an odd time that I'd want something, and she wouldn't have anticipated it.

"Ah, I caught you out," I'd say, all pleased with myself.

"Perfection is an impossibility," Jean would say.

We'd smile.

But it's such a rare occurrence, we both find it funny. Otherwise, she's too perfect.

When it comes to interacting with the children, our main age group of patients, Jean doesn't often talk to them directly. I think Jean sees her role as the support person and thus doesn't like to interfere. The primary relationship in the dental chair has to be between the dentist and the patient. I have to balance the discussion between me (the dentist), the child, and the parent. So, Jean is good like that – being the quiet, anticipating partner.

If I compare her to Cris, Cris probably chats more to the children than Jean does. Maybe the reason is because Jean doesn't remember them from one visit to the next. Jean's interactions with the children will be to sort out what they want to watch on the television. Jean does talk about movies a lot. She loves movies and is very knowledgeable about them. It's one thing she'll talk with the kids about – a good topic of conversation for her.

Sometimes, Jean talks about her writing with the patients and parents. If an opening comes up, she'll drop a hint. And if someone says, "What's your book about?" or "What is the writing contest about?" she'll then go into it. Same with the office staff. It is her passion, and it shows when she talks about it.

Jean won't remember what sport the child is playing or what school they are attending. But, if I make a note in the file, Jean will read it before the patient comes in and remember that point. Come to think of it, it might help Jean more if I put more of those social details in the notes. It might help jog her memory.

One thing I do notice about Jean that may be an effect of the Face Blindness is that she doesn't have as much physical contact with others as some people might have. We would hug if we hadn't seen each other in a couple of weeks, but we wouldn't have a lot of hugs.

I also know that she hardly ever cries. We sometimes have interesting discussions about it. Even when Jean is really down. She's not a crier. It might be related to the Face Blindness. Jean has certainly seen me cry a few times.

Because we've worked together for so long and know each other so well, we have a very close relationship and have shared difficult times in our private lives. Jean has had bereavements, ongoing family illnesses, upheavals, and serious injuries, just to name a few. During all that time, never has she shed a tear.

When Jean talks about those events, I get a sense of less emotion behind her conversation compared to others or even myself. Even if you go to work and Jean's feeling unwell, she'll never say. She'll never take the day off and won't mention it until maybe later in the day when you say, "Jean, you're not quite yourself today." Then, she'll tell me what has happened. It will be quite matter of fact. Very stark. No emotion. Just a statement. Unlike others who will go on about whatever the problem is. However, I don't know how much of that is related to the American way, that you have to go to work sick, be stoic, and hold on. It may be either way or both. Knowing what I do now, I would think it more related to the Face Blindness.

I'm not saying that there is no emotion. That's not humanly possible. I don't know if Jean feels things on the inside and doesn't betray it, or if she doesn't feel it… can't feel it. I don't mean to say that she is harsh or unfeeling, but she doesn't portray a lot of emotion. But over the years that I've known Jean, she's become more likely to share how she's feeling.

For example, when she talks about her writing, she's quite excited about it and shares it. It is visible. She's attached to her pets. I know that she cuddles them. But her passion is definitely her writing.

I normally don't think about Jean's Face Blindness. Her writing this book has jogged my memory about it and my interest. But it's certainly not something I think about on a daily or weekly basis. We just sort of carry on. And that's a good thing.

Jean does a great job of being the best person she can be and not letting it get in her way. I admire that. More people should be like that.

What does Jean say? Oh yes. It goes something like this:

"I like to try something new each year. To experience life. Because if you are not careful, life will pass you by and you'll have done very little. What a waste of an opportunity that would be."

I think that's a good motto. I'm just now discovering the wisdom behind the words myself. Live life. Experience it. Find joy in learning something new.

Jean may not remember people, even me, but you would never know because she doesn't let it get to her. She has found a way to make it work for her. That's a skill in itself. I really admire her.

Seventeen:

# Marriage – Part Two

*"The problem is not the problem. The problem is your attitude about the problem. Do you understand?"*

*Captain Jack Sparrow in* The Pirates of the Caribbean:
The Curse of the Black Pearl
*– screenplay by Ted Elliott and Terry Rossio*

Everyone has at least one pivotal point in life. It could be marriage, the birth of a child, the death of a loved one, or a revelation of some sort. Something that changes their life – large or small.

Face Blindness leaves me empty of the memory of people. It's the events, those special moments that stick with me. Thus, my marriage was a pivotal point. The birth of my first child was a pivotal point. However, they didn't change me. I was still the self-conscious person of my youth.

But something that most would consider minor became a major pivotal point in my life. It wasn't external. It was internal.

All three children were in school. My time was freed up. A career was now a possibility. I started working as a dental assistant in a busy clinic in Troy, New York. I loved the new direction my life was taking. It felt like a fresh start. I had just turned thirty.

With my twenties gone to raising young children, I started thinking about doing something for myself, something to boost my self-esteem. I had been doing craft work for years: counted cross stitch projects and crocheting from doilies to afghan blankets. Those activities in themselves make for isolation, done at home, alone.

I was looking to broaden myself, test my abilities, and break out of my comfort zone.

*A musical instrument*, I thought.

Yes, that would be new and interesting. I had always wanted to learn the guitar or the piano.

However, at the time, I had met a woman who was taking voice lessons. She told me how much she was enjoying them and how it was improving her confidence.

"Hmmm, confidence?" I inquired.

"Yes. It's amazing what it does for your self-esteem," she insisted.

"How can singing raise your self-esteem?" I asked, curious because it seemed like such a contradiction – singing in front of people.

"It gives you internal strength. Like any instrument, the more you work at it, and the better you get, you can't but help share it."

She left me the name and phone number of her teacher.

I couldn't stop thinking about what she had said. I knew my singing voice was okay. I had pitch and could carry a tune. But to sing in front of people (even if it were only the teacher), the one thing I had no connection to? That was a terrifying thought. Singing is an intimate exercise. You cannot blame an instrument for any mistakes or faults. *You* are the instrument. All the errors are yours and personal. You have to own them. Fix them. Change.

So, I did it. I made an appointment for an initial lesson.

I drove to downtown Albany, an older part of the city,

saying all the way, "What am I doing? What am I doing?" Talk about butterflies in my stomach.

The houses there were regal three-story stone structures, and very imposing with their grand windows, handsome stonework, and wrought iron fences. The street smelled of old money. It was no place for a woman like me.

I found the address and knocked on the large door. A woman opened it. Her name was MiMi O'Neill, an opera singer. I don't remember what she looked like, only that she had an air of confidence and a beautiful elegance like a ballerina dancer.

Ms. O'Neill ushered me into her impressive studio. A grand piano sat off to one side. Against one wall was the largest mirror I had ever seen. A metal music stand stood in front of the mirror. I soon learned that was where I was to stand and practice. Ms. O'Neill told me that I would come to view the mirror as a friend, just like a bodybuilder does when checking his posture and the motion of the weights.

I hated that mirror. I knew it was me in the reflection, yet it felt like a stranger. At this point, I didn't connect my discomfort to the Face Blindness. I attributed it to my insecurities.

I learned to view that person in the mirror as an object. As soon as I did that, my lessons improved.

When Ms. O'Neill first sang for me, I was floored. Her voice was amazing. Effortless. Such control and range. I wanted that!

At the time, I was making some extra money. I wanted to invest in myself. I reasoned that I deserved this opportunity.

For the first six months of lessons, I felt like a complete failure. My instrument was terrible. The person in the mirror constantly mocked me. However, Ms. O'Neill kept encouraging me, telling me that my voice would improve. There was much I had to unlearn. I had new muscles to train, new techniques to learn and master. All of those take time. So, I kept at it. Slowly I improved. With the advances came a sense of achievement. The achievement brought a growing confidence.

I heard one of Ms. O'Neill's students learning an Italian aria. I thought how beautiful she sounded. Before that, my experience with opera music had been minimal. I knew I could reach the high notes. I went home and listened to some famous arias. Though I didn't understand the language, the music moved me. I wanted to sing to move others too. So I asked Ms. O'Neill if she could teach me. She agreed that I was ready to try some of the simpler pieces. I was thrilled.

The person in the mirror somehow became my friend. My posture changed. My attitude brightened. My inner self found contentment. I became whole again. All from learning to sing.

I stayed with Ms. O'Neill for a year and a half. At that time, the print shop Uwe worked at was going under. With printers closing their doors throughout New York State, we started looking for work further south. Uwe's parents' health had stabilized. We packed up again and headed to Hampton, Virginia, where Uwe accepted a job offer.

I found a voice teacher soon after we settled in: Patricia Ricciarelli. (I've gone through my files. I tend to keep everything. That's how I can write down my teachers' names.) I stayed with her for five years.

When we moved to New Zealand, I found another teacher in Hamilton, Audrey Paterson. I studied with Mrs. Paterson for two years before she died from a stroke. I haven't picked it up since. I still consider myself an amateur when it comes to singing. However, the lessons had served an important purpose. I had learned to be confident and content with the person I was.

~

In America, the southern folks were so different from the north. They are more open to emotion, good and bad. They are very hospitable; that southern hospitality is an actual thing. I'm not much into fried chicken and greens, but until you've had them home-cooked by a southerner, you have no clue what you've been missing. The southern folk aren't so inhibited. New Yorkers can be stuffy at times. (I can say that freely because I'm a New Yorker, born and raised.)

My husband loved to entertain. Soon after we settled in the south, we were putting on entertainment nights… talent shows, but without the pressure. Good old-fashion fun. We would include music, dances, skits, jokes, and of course, singing. We ended up doing a skit each year. They were hilarious and great fun. I loved doing them because I could become someone else for a brief time.

One year, we did a parody of the *Three Little Pigs* called *Three Pigs of Small Stature,* done in the manner of a Chinese proverb. I was the little pig that built the wooden house made of bamboo. The next year we did a spoof of *Gitarzan*, a Ray Steven's song. I made my brother Jeff a crazy Tarzan costume that he bravely wore. He was a skinny beanpole and looked ridiculous. I still have that picture, which is how I know. I was Jane. Again, we had great fun.

While we were putting the acts for the show together, I decided, *Yup, I've practiced long enough. I'm going to sing something for the show.*

I carefully chose an aria, one that wasn't too taxing and had no problematic shifts in the midrange. I had made a Renaissance gown of maroon velvet and rose satin. It was the most beautiful thing I've ever sewn. Backstage, I changed from Jane and into the dress and instantly became another person. I walked out, nerves making my mouth dry. I couldn't remember a single word. I freaked out. Then the music played. I took a deep breath. Opened my mouth. And sang.

It was the scariest and best thing I've ever done. I don't remember getting through it, but I do remember the applause.

Afterward, everyone came up to me with amazement and praise. They would never have guessed that was in me. A couple years back and I never would've imagined it either.

It was the icebreaker to my shy soul.

After that, I sang at some other gatherings, growing more confident each time I got up in front of a group. I don't remember who was there. Always a sea of faces, whether a few or many. Always forgotten.

That pivotal point of starting voice lessons changed me as a person. I was someone new, reborn. It changed my perspective on life. I was now confident in my skin. I didn't need confirmation from the outside world anymore. That was *huge*. I realized that I could be happy with myself in a world of no faces. I didn't need to rely on other people for internal peace or acceptance. Yes, this new realization came from singing. And *that* was the purpose of all those lessons.

It was a good thing that I had built some inner strength, for my life was about to change. A storm was on the horizon. None of us saw it coming. My anchor, my one constant, was about to break.

~

One day in the autumn of 2003, I came home during my lunch break and found Uwe in a state.

"What's wrong?" I asked.

Uwe broke down and cried. Hard! I'd never seen him like this before. It was scary. I tried to comfort him but to no avail. He wouldn't speak. Just raw emotion. He was like that for an hour. I finally had to go back to work. It was on my mind all afternoon. Uwe worked second shift, so I didn't see him again until the next day, though I did call him that evening to see if he wanted to talk but he said he was okay. The next day when I saw him at lunch, I asked him if he was stressed because he had too much on his plate. He was working long hours and had many other responsibilities within our church. Including family obligations, there was little time left for himself.

The fixer in me was desperate to find a way to fix whatever was wrong with my husband. I had no clue as to what was wrong. It wasn't until three years later that the truth came out.

Soon after that incident, Uwe was back to normal. I had put the incident aside and soon forgot about it. By December, he was talking about moving again. This time to the far west – Idaho, Washington, Oregon – and further: Australia.

"Australia?" I said, surprised by his enthusiasm for the idea.

We had moved so much that it was second nature to me. To have roots in one spot was a foreign concept. It probably had something to do with my disconnection from people. Usually, it's your relationship with family and friends that keep you grounded in a spot. So, when Uwe grew excited about a possible move again, I took it all in my stride.

Australia sounded interesting. When I started researching the possibility of emigrating to that fascinating country, it became a viable option. I loved the idea of the adventure, not realizing that Uwe might have had an ulterior motive for the move.

But we never made it to Australia. While I was doing that research, the movies *Lord of the Rings*: *The Fellowship of the Ring* and *The Two Towers* were released. I had grown up reading Tolkien's novels and had fantasized about Middle Earth as a child. To see the story come alive on the big screen was fulfilling a dream. It took my breath away. My children will tell you that I was a little obsessive about it at the time. I have to sheepishly agree. Why not? They were amazing films. And the scenery… Words can't describe how stunning the mountains, valleys, and clear waters were. When I realized that the amazing scenery for the movies was shot in a little-known country called New Zealand, I was intrigued.

Within a year, we were living in New Zealand in the heart of 'The Shire,' thirty-five minutes from the Hobbiton set. I was living where my teenage self had dreamed of being.

Before we made the final decision, Uwe, Logan (our oldest son), and I went for a month-long visit. I had lined up job interviews for Uwe in Hamilton and Wellington on the North Island. Halfway through the trip, when Uwe had been offered a job in Hamilton, we decided to make the move. We had seen and learned enough to make an informed decision.

Uwe called the print shop and accepted their offer. Logan and I went back to the States, while Uwe stayed in New Zealand to start the immigration process, find us a home, and begin work. Back home, I sold the house, arranged international shipping of our stuff, and gathered all the necessary documents for immigration. It was no small feat. There were problems along the way, some very difficult, that I had to handle on my own. But I did it. Was I ever glad when we finally landed in Auckland!

What about the family? Mom? Dad? Siblings? Friends? Yes, I left them all behind. Even my eldest son, Logan. It's funny when I think back on it; I didn't shed a tear. Nor did I have any longing for my family, even my son. No homesickness. Nothing.

I couldn't understand why the others pined for the family.

"We are on the grandest adventure of our life," I'd say to them. "Concentrate on this new country, the beauty, the culture. That should fill your days and hearts."

I was clueless about their pain, for I felt nothing for those we left behind.

Once we became immersed in our new life, their homesickness faded. Skype was set up and regularly used to see and talk to family members in the States. It was and still is a necessity for the others.

But I don't need to see family. I need to hear their voices to have any sense of connection.

We were far from home and in a strange country. The stress of the move was the most difficult for Uwe. We didn't realize there was an underlying issue. The symptoms were subtle at first: a lack of interest in everyday things, growing isolation, and paranoia – questioning everything I was doing, where I was going, who I was with. That sort of thing. It got so bad that I didn't want to be around him anymore. It was easier to keep my distance.

Our communication suffered. Finally, after putting up with Uwe's odd behavior for two years, I asked him to get help – for him and for us. I explained how much his behavior was hurting me. How I felt like a bruised flower in a desert, trying hard to survive. This was our marriage I was talking about. It was during this conversation that he finally admitted what had happened way back when he broke down that day I came home during my lunch break.

"Were you having an affair with Dr. Leigh?" he asked.

Dr. Leigh was the dentist I was working for before the big move.

I was shocked. Speechless! I'd never entertained such a thought. Never in all our years of marriage. Didn't Uwe understand? I don't *see* people. I don't *need* people. What would I need with an affair? I couldn't fathom it. What had happened to Uwe?

Finally, it came out.

"The day before, I went to your office at lunch, and it was all locked up. Your car was there. So was his," Uwe reluctantly explained.

I couldn't believe his excuse. It made me sick inside.

"We lock up the office every day at lunch," I said. "It's standard practice. Everyone was in the break room in the back. Why didn't you ring the bell?"

Uwe had no answer. Yet he still believed I had been unfaithful. And not just with Dr. Leigh but with others before him.

I was floored. I was hurt. Then, I was angry. It hit me that here was the reason Uwe wanted to move, not just within the States, but as far away as he could get me. I don't know if he was even conscious of that fact.

"What about Ben?" Uwe demanded.

"What about Ben?" I said.

"Don't tell me that you don't have feelings for him."

"He's a friend. Nothing more."

"I don't believe you."

"Go ask him yourself. Go ask all the people we hang out with."

"I will!"

And he did. He came back with nothing, but the damage to our relationship was already done.

"Is that what you really think of me?" I said. "After all these years? I have never been unfaithful to you. Never! You need help. Go see a doctor before it's too late. You need to fix this. Now."

I didn't explain what I meant by 'before it's too late,' but it was enough for him to finally see a doctor.

I knew there had been something physically wrong with Uwe for some time. Heart palpitations and a trembling of his hands, plus the paranoia and personality change all pointed to Grave's disease. Sure enough, that's what it was. It took two more difficult years before he finally agreed to have the necessary surgery. Once he had his thyroid removed and was on medication, the physical symptoms stopped, and his temperament improved.

However, the damage to our marriage was not so easily fixed.

Face Blindness may take memories away of people and the mix of emotions that come with people. But when you live with someone and see him every day, hear their voice – that pain, the hurt they caused, doesn't go away. The injurious words stick.

I wear a mask most days. Whenever I'm in a group or meeting people, the smile is in place. I don't know who is who until I have had time to figure out where they fit in my life. I have to pretend that I know them. It's as natural for me to put on this mask as it is to put on clothes in the morning.

As soon as I was home, the mask came off. It wasn't needed. I knew I could be who I was without repercussions.

Not anymore.

From that day, when my marriage started to crumble, I put on the mask.

~

For a while, things returned to a sense of normality. Uwe improved, though our marriage remained on shifting sand. He wanted what we had had before, but the innocence and trust were broken. I told him the damage he inflicted was deep, and it would take time for me to recover. Internally, I was thinking about how easy it would be to walk away. I would forget him soon enough, like everyone else. But I believe firmly in marriage vows – in *our* marriage vows. If Uwe could be patient with me, we might be able to weather this storm and come through. I desperately needed my anchor back.

During this time, I started my writing career. Initially, I used it as an excuse to spend time away from Uwe. It was a place where I could sink into my own worlds, a place where I was in complete control. It was exhilarating and, simultaneously, therapeutic. I fell in love with the creative process. It brought me great joy, substituting for what was missing in our marriage.

I'm not going to lie: my newfound love for writing was rocky going. One minute, Uwe was supportive, even excited. The next minute, he was upset with me, telling me that he didn't want me writing. During those times, I wrote in secret, picking my times carefully so as not to harm our already shaky relationship. I knew it wasn't fair on his part, putting me in that position, but I so wanted to try to fix us.

When the first book of *The Vault Agency* series was finished and in Uwe's hands, he was so proud. It was like he had forgotten all the times he hated my writing.

*Maybe now, he will like that I write,* I thought, *see that it's a real thing for me.*

Uwe wanted to be involved and came up with all sorts of ways to help me. I responded with all the right replies, but in my heart, I knew it wouldn't last. By this time, I was used to his rollercoaster responses. And he didn't disappoint me.

We went on like this for a time.

As my writing progressed, I decided to make it a career. I'd been doing dentistry for ten years. The transition would not be overnight. I knew that and made plans accordingly. When we had moved to New Zealand, and I started working with a pediatric dental specialist, our rooms were located within an oral/maxillary surgeons' practice. This led me to expand my skills into oral surgery, which I love. I was working twenty to twenty-five hours a week at the practice. Fitting the writing around that schedule wasn't too difficult once it was down on paper. My husband was on board with the schedule, and so I thought all was okay.

It was, for a brief time. But old habits are quickly remembered. Though I was happy while I was writing away, Uwe was not. Little did I realize that the Grave's disease was not the only problem.

Our children married. Soon, the grandchildren arrived. Usually, it's me that has a lack of interest in people. But it's different with my children. They belong to me. I may not feel it emotionally, but logic tells me that those relationships are important, just as my marriage is important.

With Uwe's temperament as fickle as an island breeze, it made it difficult to be around him. The family noticed. We stopped having friends over for dinner. We stopped doing things together, planning trips together, spending time together. It was easier that way and safer for me, emotionally and mentally.

For years, I made excuses for Uwe's behavior, sometimes lying for him to protect him from what others would think. For years, I was the strong one, holding the family together, hiding Uwe's psychotic behavior from the world.

Not anymore.

There comes the point, even for someone like me who cannot remember much associated with a person, where the mind and the heart cannot cope. What I held to believe as a healthy relationship was gone, shattered by years and years of strain and neglect. I don't put all the accountability on Uwe. I know my disorder has not helped the situation. Though Uwe says he understands, he really doesn't.

How do I know this? Because he no longer considers how he talks to me. His voice has changed. His mannerisms have changed. A stranger sleeps in my bed. How can I let him touch me? It feels wrong. Uwe doesn't understand. How can he? I don't recognize the man I married, and it scares me.

Yet, I can't fully blame Uwe for the situation we are in at the moment. Face Blindness makes it difficult to have a deep connection that most people take for granted. It takes two people who share that emotional bond to make a relationship work. It's amazing ours has done as well as it has.

It has been recently pointed to me that Uwe has always been a stranger to me. That took me aback. I keep referring to him as my anchor, when, in reality, I have no anchor.

Others, when separated from their partner, find it difficult to be apart. When they come together, there is great joy and relief. One person described it as 'a desperation just to hold that person and not wanting to let go.' That's because they have retained a picture/image/vision/memory of their loved one and that stays with them. Severe Face Blindness takes that ability away from me. I've mentioned several times that when Uwe and I have been apart, I felt nothing for him, that he was a stranger. It wasn't Uwe that was the problem: it was me.

When difficulties come up, and they do, others can draw from the good times that they've shared, even bad times that they have weathered together.

The same person who described the joy and relief of being reunited also commented that when times are difficult, the shared memories and shared achievements, such as raising children and experiencing together the good and the bad in life, provide things to cling to. They also are shackles that can't be easily cast off when times get difficult. Simultaneously, those memories helped him to forgive and be forgiven for whatever had driven 'them' apart.

I have no memory of people, not even my husband nor children. I can't remember the good times. I can't remember the shared times. I can't remember because I lack the connection in my brain to retrieve that information. Whereas, my husband remembers everything. I have to accept the fact that Uwe, though my husband for many years, will always be somewhat of a stranger to me, and that's okay. I can cope with that. He has had his share of coping with me too, and I have to remind myself of that.

There is always hope. I try not to dwell on our marriage

problems. I remain positive; that is my personality. I concentrate on making plans and working towards their fulfillment. I apply myself to improving my life, whether it's internally or externally. These things keep me focused on a positive future and the joy that can be found in each day.

Happiness is what you make of it. I chose to make it mine and without reservations.

Eighteen:

# Emotions/Feelings

*"Emotions play out in the theater of the body. Feelings play out in the theater of the mind."*

Your Brain Health *by Dr. Sarah McKay*

Behavior is governed by the expectations of society. Feelings driven by emotions, one of the basic elements of behavior, are not so easily governed. Why? Because, as Dr. Sarah McKay put it, emotions are an integral component of our bodies. They are programmed into our DNA.

The mind, however, is not so easily explained. Within the twisted gray matter is where emotions, memories, and thinking ability meld together to create feelings. We love. We hate. We cry with delight at weddings. We cry with grief at funerals. We feel joy at the birth of a child, at meeting old friends. Fond memories surface from time to time. A sense of nostalgia grows for people that have passed through our lives, for the places we've been and the feelings that transpired from both. Layers of memories laced with emotions, some good, others bad. All proof that we have lived.

Memories.

Not just any memory, but the memories of the people who have touched our lives.

How does one with Face Blindness hold onto those memories that color our lives? Memories of people and all that entails? That which enriches us as a person?

We don't. Oh, yes, they are stored inside our minds, but they're irretrievable. Sometimes, when I think about it, it makes me angry.

It's not fair. I want to be normal. I want to remember!

The lack of connection that comes from memories leaves me feeling alone. I have no recall of anyone, or very little. Whether with family, friends, or workmates, wherever I am, I am alone. And that hurts.

Most of the time, I can ignore the pain. I can go through each day and not dwell on it. Weeks can pass. I can plaster a smile on my face and pretend to be like everyone else. Inside, I know that I'm not. But sooner or later, Face Blindness will rear up and shake my inner resolve not to care.

Approaching the topic of emotions versus feelings and their subsequent relationship to Face Blindness is difficult for me. I already know that I'm not like others. I think differently; I behave somewhat differently. Unveiling the why behind that behavior leaves me feeling exposed to the cruelness of the world. Who wants to admit that they are peculiar? Even alien-like?

Nonetheless, I cannot justify leaving the most integral part of what makes us human out of this book. It wouldn't be fair to you, the reader. So, I must press forward and do my best to help you comprehend the complexities. It's important to me because emotional-memory ties (or lack of those ties) are a vital part of understanding the whole nature of Face Blindness.

In scientific terms, emotions are lower level responses occurring in the subcortical regions of the brain (the amygdala) and the ventromedial prefrontal cortices, creating biochemical reactions in your body, altering your physical state. Emotions are coded in our genes and are universally similar across the human race.

Emotions precede feelings. They are physical and instinctive. They are chemical reactions to certain stimuli. Because they are physical, they can be objectively measured by blood flow, brain activity, facial micro-expressions, and body language. Emotions can be scientifically documented.

On the other hand, feelings are much more fluid.

"Feelings are mental experiences of body states, which arise as the brain interprets emotions. (The order of such events is: I am threatened, I experience fear, then I feel horror.)"[3]

In plain words, feelings are formed from emotions mixed with thoughts, memories, and images that have subconsciously linked with that particular emotion. These emotions accumulate over time, and our brain turns them into feelings. While the emotions may be temporary, the feelings they evoke may persist and grow with time.

For example, you meet a new classmate. Something about that person draws you. You start to hang out together. By the end of the school year, you are best friends. Years go by. You've shared good times. You've shared bad times. Then you move away. Yet, those feelings of closeness never leave you. Even years later, when you meet up, all those memories surface, and it's like you've never been apart.

For someone with severe Face Blindness, this scenario is highly unlikely because of the faulty recall mechanisms in their brain.

Studies in the Netherlands and at Massachusetts General Hospital lead by Beatrice de Gelder shows that the presence of emotional information in the face increases neural activity

---

[3] MIT Technology Review: The Importance of Feelings by Jason Pontin, June 17, 2014. Interview with Antonio D'Amasio, professor of neuroscience at The University of California.

in the area of the brain associated with face recognition. The scientist explained that the emotion in a face carries important communicative information, making it vital as a reading tool to the person with Face Blindness.

However, feelings, as discussed, go deeper than an emotional response on a face. The problem still exists – making a connection with past memories of a person and drawing them together to formulate a structure for emotional growth.

When I was a little girl, my older sister, Yvonne, and I used to visit my aunt during summer vacation and school holidays. The visit would last for a week. My aunt worked at a nursing home on the night shift. Sometimes we would go with her for a few hours until her roommate got off work and picked us up. Lights were turned down. Creepy noises seeped from behind half-shut doors. We'd eat chocolate pudding and race down the empty halls in wheelchairs, making up scary stories about the old people. It was fun.

My aunt knew a lot of elderly people. It seemed like on every visit, we were at someone's funeral. My sister didn't take it well, crying and carrying on even after we returned home. I, on the other hand, felt quite detached from the whole 'death' thing. They weren't humans, just figures. I was pretty proud of myself. Little did I know that there was a reason for my detachment.

The detachment from people showed up many times during my youth and into adulthood. The first time I started to question my emotional state was when I had children. Other mothers would talk about the bond that instantly formed between them and their newborn baby. I never felt that. Even while pregnant, I would say that the growing fetus was an alien thing inside me.

I'm not saying that I was a bad mother. My children will tell you today that I was a very good mother. However, I never felt motherly. I took care of them. Fed them. Bathed them. Played with them. Taught them. But I never felt attached to them. They will jokingly tell you that my method of motherhood was more of a military boot camp. Oh yes, I told them, 'I love you' and gave them affection. I didn't want them to go through the same feelings of loneliness that I had experienced growing up. I made sure I was always there for them. It was my duty. My obligation as a mother. But it wasn't based on love.

Honestly, I don't think I love anyone. I don't truly understand what love is.

Think about it. What is loved based on? You don't love someone just because. Love is a feeling based on building blocks of shared experiences – of memories. I don't have these at my disposal.

I had struggled alone with this inner turmoil for years until one day when I was visiting Jeff, my youngest brother. We fell into a discussion about love. He also struggles with recognition.

"What do you think about love?" Jeff asked.

"What do you mean?" I replied.

"I don't think I feel love."

The loss and loneliness in his voice brought tears to my eyes. He expressed what I could not.

"I don't think I do either," I finally admitted.

To say it out loud and to someone who understood was such a relief. We talked for a long time on the subject, comparing our experiences around Face Blindness. He confirmed what I had already figured out; our emotional attachment to people is limited… if it exists at all.

For example, most people love their mother. There are cases of those who have had an abusive mother, but in general, this is not the norm. Mothers are almost universally known to be loving and nurturing in nature.

My mother was no different. To this day, she gives one hundred percent of herself to other people, including her children. By all standards of the definition, I should love her. There's no reason for me not to. Do I love her? No. I can't even remember her. All memories of my childhood and adulthood are devoid of people, including my wonderful mother.

It's not that I don't know that I have a mother and that she is still alive. Those are the facts. It's the emotional tie that I'm lacking. It's the building blocks of shared memories. My mother is a stranger to me. A loving stranger. Her facial expressions, body language, and voice tell me that we are intimately connected. I take this information in and treat it as fact. When we are together, I don't say that I am pretending to care or share affection. However, once I am away, it's all forgotten – those feelings along with the person.

Blink, and she's gone. That simple.

Admitting this is not easy. Even now, while I sit here and type it, I feel the stigma, I sense of the glares of those who don't understand.

I do recognize my mother's voice when we talk on Skype. I will remember the things we did together, but only when they are brought up. I am fully aware that I *should* feel something for her. That's what makes it so painful: knowing this yet not feeling it.

I dare not express this to others, let alone to my mother, that I feel no love. First, she wouldn't understand it. Second, there is no point to her knowing. It is better for her to remain ignorant of my deficiency than to carry the burden that the knowledge would hold.

It is the same with my children. It was especially evident to me when we moved away, and I no longer had constant interactions with them.

Though they are the most important people in my life,

they are forgotten just as quickly as the checkout person at the grocery counter. I feel nothing. No sense of longing. No need for affection from them. No homesickness. Nothing.

I go about my daily life as if these people never existed. It makes me sad when I think about it, especially when I hear others talk so passionately about their children, close family members, and friends. It's not that I don't know that I have children and family. It's just that they are not in my head. No memory building blocks. Thus, no deep feelings.

A couple of years back, I had an innocent admirer. He was a teenager with autism. It wasn't me particularly that he liked. It was because I was from America and knew about Native Americans. That was his fascination. Every week at our religious meetings, he would seek me out to talk about the Indians and the one-dollar bill he kept in his wallet. Unexpectedly, he died. He was twenty-one. My husband and I were first to the house. He lived with his parents. I cried with his mother. I cried at the funeral. And then… nothing.

The next day, I was back to my usual self. I had no memory of the face of this young man. I never did. I couldn't recall his name though I had interactions with him for three years. All the emotions of the day before were gone. I went on with my life as if he had never existed. Even now, when others bring up memories of him in conversation, I *feel* neutral. Not good or bad. Just nothing.

Uwe used to tease me and say, "You're the perfect woman."

"Thank you. But I'm not. I've got this brain thing," I'd reply.

And we'd both laughed. It became an ongoing joke.

My family, also, jokingly say that I am an alien. Not just because I'm always seeking a heat source (like a lizard), but that I react to situations like a Vulcan. *Spockette* was a favorite nickname given to me. Always logical and practical. I used to be proud of the fact that I wasn't an emotional person. Now, I know better, understanding the reason behind the detachment.

If you ask the kids how many times they have seen me cry, they will count them off:

"When the dogs destroyed the ornamental garden pond Mom had just completed."

"When Alex, Mom's cat, died."

And, most recently, "When Mom had called a meeting with us kids to ask for help with Dad."

Three times in twenty-five years. That's not normal. Even I have to admit that. Though I have cried at a couple of funerals and have shed a tear or two on a few other occasions. Still, it's not enough to feel human.

You can understand why my children think me unnatural and call me an alien. Or why others consider me to be cold and unfeeling. I don't want to be this way. I yearn to be normal, to feel that deep attachment to someone. I long to know what love feels like from deep within – the kind they portray in the movies. I want to yearn to be with family, my children, and friends.

On a positive note, Face Blindness does carry certain advantages. I don't hold a grudge. How can I when I can't recall a person? I don't hate anyone or harbor any adverse feelings. I don't carry any emotional baggage from past hurts. It rolls out of my mind as easily as taking a shower and washing the mud off.

I am, for the most part, genuinely in a good mood. My mind isn't filled with conflicts.

This doesn't mean that I don't have moments of hurt or remembered emotional pain inflicted by someone. The strength of that memory depends greatly on the duration of emotional trauma or the deepness of the hurt. Even then, under extreme circumstances, those, too, will quickly fade and be forgotten.

Overall, these conditions lead one to be even-tempered.

Uwe used to tell me, "You never get upset. You're always levelheaded. Non-confrontational. Always willing to compromise."

How much of that is due to the disorder, I can only guess. But it's true. I don't feel the emotions that drive most women – most people. No ups and downs. The things that are normal to feel. Sometimes I think that makes me boring.

Some of my writer friends have asked how I can write emotions in characters if I don't have the ability to truly understand feelings. It's part guesswork and part planning. I try to find words to express what I think the character must be feeling. I've had a lot of practice playing with words in my make-believe worlds. Also, I'm good at observing human nature, whether in real life or from television and movies. The logical part of me will break down a scene to see what made it emotional. Very clinical. Why did it move me? What did they do? How did they behave? You can call it a concentrated analytical approach to emotional reactions. I use this knowledge to build believable character emotional responses when I write.

I knew I was doing something right because readers have come back and said things like, "This book is really good. I love so-and-so. I'm really attached to him or her."

Or, "Why did you kill him off? I really liked him."

Or, "When are you going to write the next book? I need to know what happens to so-and-so. There has to be more."

I use the same approach in real life, analyzing *why* people are behaving the way they are or doing what they are doing. Finding the logic behind the emotions expressed. I often make mistakes, because sometimes there is no logic to the emotion or the reason behind it is hidden.

Writing is different from real life. The writer controls the environment and the physical, mental, and emotional paths of the characters. The real world is much more complicated and cannot be contrived. When it comes to feeling emotions, this is where I falter.

It has come up in conversation, recently, about whether I love God. Ooh, a touchy subject. It was hard enough to admit to this person that I don't feel love, not even for those close to me. So, how do I approach this sensitive subject?

I tried to explain it this way:

"I may not feel love for God. But I am a logical person. Creation tells me there is an intelligence behind the design. Prophecies fulfilled require a being of greater power than us. His purpose for humans makes sense to me. On that basis alone, it is enough for me to say, 'Yes, there is a God.' And, 'Yes, He is worth worshipping.' I don't need love as my motivation, though it would be nice to have. Logic is my compass. It doesn't make me less devoted than someone who can love."

I can see on their faces the confusion as I explain.

"I'm good. Don't worry about me," I say, to comfort them.

It's strange how they need comforting when I'm the one who is suffering.

Anyway, at that point, I will turn the conversation to a safer subject – like the weather. Relief washes over their faces, reaffirming that they weren't ready for that bit of information.

I've learned to keep my relationship with God private, even when someone is curious enough to ask. It's easier to let those who know me think that I feel love for God just as they do.

It hasn't been easy, especially lately, since I've become vocal about Face Blindness and how it affects me. I've had to explain the emotional aspect of Face Blindness and the difficulties. It's still hard for people to comprehend. You can appreciate why I don't like to reveal the depth of my limitations.

"How can you not love? Your own children? Your parents? What about your husband?

These are the most frequent responses I get.

Others think I'm joking, or worse, lying about the severity of my condition. These are people who I trusted enough to confide in. I'm left wondering what the response of the general public would be.

And yet, I have told you. Why? Because I want you, even if you don't understand it, to rise above the problem and embrace me as I am. Don't question the disorder. Learn about it and work with it.

I *want* meaningful relationships. I *want* to be loved even if I cannot give back as deeply. If you commit to me, I *will* be just as committed. I believe in loyalty and commitment. I will give one hundred percent of what I can give.

For many years, none of the family knew that I had Face Blindness and they loved me as I was. They didn't question my behavior. Oh yes, they may joke about it, but all in good fun. Even if you asked them now, they would say that I love them. Maybe I do, in my odd sort of way. I don't know. Behavior can be learned.

The logical part of me helped me be a good mother, a devoted wife, and a great employee. I may not feel love or have any strong emotional ties, yet I can express real compassion and kindness. I can be a listening ear and I have a helpful nature. I do care. I am limited by a broken connection in the brain. I need others to be the bridge for me. Remind me. Fill in the gaps. I will respond.

# Nineteen:

# Helpful Tips

*"Life is locomotion. If you're not moving, you're not living. But there comes a time when you've got to stop running away from things and you've got to start running towards something. You've got to forge ahead. Keep moving even if your path isn't clear. Trust that you'll find your way."*

*Barry Allen, DC Comics* The Flash *Volume 4, #1 (2011)*

There was once a great captain of a spaceship called the Enterprise. His name was Captain Jean Luc Picard. Though he was firm, as a captain should be, he showed great wisdom and understanding of human nature.

Now, I know Captain Picard isn't a real person but a fictional character. However, there was something he said that, at the time, I felt compelled to write in my book of quotes.

He said, "Time is a companion that goes with us on a journey. It reminds us to cherish each moment because it will never come again. What we leave behind is not as important as how we have lived."

Looking back, I didn't understand the significance of that little speech. Now, with my eyes open to the realities of living with Face Blindness, I can see why I had written it down.

Living each day for that day, cherishing each moment as

it happens, not dwelling on the past. No recall of yesteryears but living for the journey ahead. That pretty much sums up Face Blindness as I have experienced it.

It's not a bad journey compared to some. My 'road' has taken me on an alternate route. And yet, I know that I am loved. I have a family. I have friends. There are people whom I cannot recall. I have learned to consider them my friends as well.

I have a motto: Try one new thing each year.

It's ironic because most of the things I've done through the years have involved other people in some way or another. Theater, singing, dance, scuba diving, just to name a few. You would think it would be easier to isolate myself. I won't lie: that would seem to be the obvious option. But I don't like easy. I like to challenge myself. It has helped me cope with Face Blindness and the loneliness associated with the disorder.

So, that's enough about me.

What have you learned so far?

Face Blindness is a cognitive disorder, where the ability to recognize faces, including one's own face (self-recognition), is impaired. The impairment can include the inability to recall memories associated with a person or people.

The disorder affects two percent of the population. That two percent fall on a spectrum that ranges from mild to severe. A person is either born with the disorder or gets it due to head trauma or a stroke. People who have it due to trauma are immediately aware of the difference, whereas those born with Face Blindness are not aware that they have it and may learn of it later as an adult. Studies on the disorder are still relatively new, and at the writing of this book, information on the subject is still limited.

What can you do if you learn someone you know has Face Blindness?

1) Say your name each time you meet. Don't assume they will remember it even if you're a family member.

2) Remind them of how you are connected to them. "I am your friend." "I am your boss." "I am from (fill in the blank)." This is of vital importance, especially when you meet out of context.

3) Remind them of where you last were together, or if it was a phone call, or Skype, etc. It's called an 'event.' They may not 'see' you in the event/memory, but they will recall the place and will put you in it.

4) Remind them of what you last talked about. This, too, is an anchor point. If you use both three and four, they most likely have enough information to know who you are, where you fit in their life, and to feel relatively comfortable.

5) When they walk into a group or gathering, remember that to them, everyone is a stranger until they can process who is who through voice recognition and anchor points leaked through conversations. So, make it easier for them by going to them and doing the above four steps.

6) Talk. They will learn your voice pattern as you converse with them. The more you talk, the more they will get to know the pattern. They will use your voice (plus body posturing and mannerisms) instead of your face to recognize who you are.

7) They honestly want to be your friend. It means that you have to do more work in initiating things. Such as calling or texting and reminding them of your friendship. It's not that they don't want you as a friend; it's just that they can't remember that you are their friend. Don't give up on them. They need you. I promise that the extra effort is worth it.

If you can do the above, you will bring relief and joy to those who go through life feeling like an outsider when with people.

~

I hope that opening up about the disorder through the telling of my experience will help enlighten those interested in, or affected by, the subject. In writing this book, I have aimed at different groups of people.

First, it is for others who suffer from Face Blindness. To help affirm that they are not alone with the problem and that someone else understands what they are going through. How they feel about loneliness and a lack of connection or attachment to people is normal for us. As you can see from my life, we can function in society, even flourish. My desire is to give such people hope and inspiration.

Second, it is for the family members who are trying to understand but are finding it difficult. I hope that after reading this book, it will unlock the way for honest, non-judgmental conversations between the sufferer and their loved ones. May you work to find ways to ease their daily struggle to place people, even with someone who may only nominally be affected.

Third, to the general public, I hope that reading this book will bring some understanding of the subject to light. Even if you can't quite get your head around the disorder and its effects on the sufferer, I hope that, if you know someone or should meet someone with Face Blindness, you will know what to expect and maybe help them out a bit. I can guarantee that it will be much appreciated.

None of us should judge people because they may not behave as society expects. We don't know what may be affecting people, why they do what they do, or why they act 'oddly.' Treat everyone with kindness, and don't presume to know. Life is too short. Let's make it as uncomplicated as we can.

Knowledge is the key. Wisdom is the vehicle. Love is the driving force.

I may not recognize your face. I cannot 'see' it. I know

what I have to do to cope. That is my knowledge.

I've now shared what I know with you. That is my wisdom.

I will continue to share my experience and knowledge of Face Blindness to make it easier for me and for others like me. That is my driving force.

Do you have the driving force to spare? The love? Then, share it and make our world of no faces one that we with Face Blindness can see.

# Acknowledgements

It took several years to get this book to the point of publication. Many people were involved in the process, donating their time and energy to make it happen.

First and foremost, I want to thank Lewis Morgan, the project coordinator, for his endless enthusiasm, the many hours spent in organizing and conducting the interviews, and for his insightful observations. It was only by his constant prodding that I got this work off the ground and into something tangible.

I thank all those who were interviewed: Uwe Scherle, Dan Carroll, Katie Ayers, Jeff Gilbert, and Lewis Morgan. Their observations and perceptions not only enlightened me and broadened my perspective, but also will help others get a better understanding of the disorder and how it affects those who live, work, and associate closely with someone who has Face Blindness.

The foreword was graciously provided by a fellow Face Blindness sufferer. Thank you, Lauren, for your inciteful comments and interest in this book.

Thank you to my great editor, Chad Dick of 100% Proof Ltd, for his patience, sensitivity to the subject material, his behind the scenes advice, and for pulling the manuscript into its final form.

I want to thank you, the reader, for taking an interest in the subject. You will be surprised, for someday, you will actually get to use the information when you come across someone like me. They will thank you for your understanding, as I thank you now.